Howto for Windows and Internet Virgins.

The Basics in Using a Windows Computer.

Protection, Maintenance, Programs and their Use, etc.

Using Windows XP and Vista.

Also how the Internet works and how you can use the Internet.

Author Bill Rosoman Dip CS

Published by Bill Rosoman Dip CS

Copies of this book can be ordered from

www.lulu.com/leftfieldnz

First Published 2009

ISBN 978-0-473-14757-0

Table of Contents

Introduction

Over the years I have made many manuals, handbooks and howtos for the use of Computers, It is hard to remember (I have been using computers since the early 1980s), that there are still plenty of Windows and Internet Virgins OUT THERE! Also they are not just young people, but of all ages. Some have had a little experience but completely do not understand the technology or the use and maintenance of computers.

This Howto is an attempt to assist in curing that state of affairs. An attempt to Break your Virginity LOL!

Please do some computer basics as suggested in this Howto.

But above all else have fun OUT THERE!

Relax it is cool OUT THERE!

About the Author

I lived and worked for Post Office/Telecom and then myself on the East Coast, above Gisborne, of the North Island of New Zealand for 29 years.

From 2002 to the present I am working, and living in a Campervan, in the Hamilton/Waikato Region of New Zealand with many trips in the region and the North Island.

I have a life long interest in electronics. I built my first crystal set radio in the 1960s. I got my first computer in the early 1980s.

My interest in Windows and Linux has been for many years now and it is fun, and very interesting. While I am not a programmer I have contributed by doing documentation and providing assistance were I can. It certainly keeps the brain active and it is great that a lot of free open source software is community supported.

Bill Rosoman Dip CS

February 2009

Understanding Technology

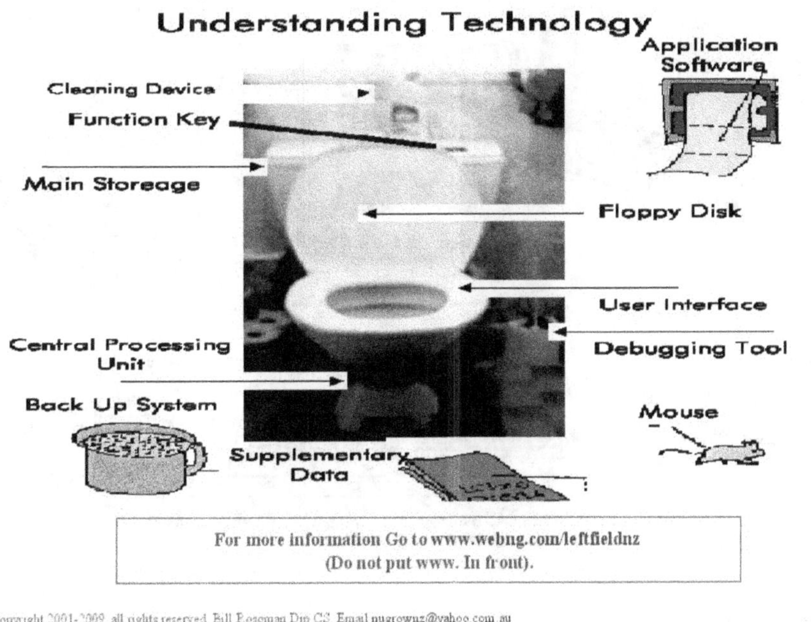

See it is REAL Easy!

The biggest thing about computers, is to give it a go and to try something new.

It is very hard to destroy a computer or the software that drives it during normal use.

As long as you follow a few simply rules and do a bit of house keeping on your Computer you should be fine.

If things go really wrong turn off the computer and go and have a coffee, it is probably something real simple that will fix the problem!

But above all have a bit of fun.

I use Computers to a lot of their potential and am self-taught, Press a few buttons and see what happens.

The Windows Operating System

Windows what a beast! Personally I avoid it like the plague and only use Linux Kubuntu www.kubuntu.org Kubuntu Operating System is all legal and free and does not get viruses or spyware, but that is another story.

Windows needs a lot of user intervention in keeping it up to date, free of viruses and spyware and well tuned so you do not have problems down the track

Maintenance and Backups should be done on a regular basis perhaps weekly or monthly. It depends on how much you use the computer and how paranoid you are LOL.

There is no reason to buy software. Most the suggested software in this Howto is free and legal software.

There is a table in this Howto of all the suggested free software available for most computer users needs.

Two programs you should never use in Windows are Windows Internet Explorer and Outlook Express Email. They are just shocking programs IMHO.

I recommend Open Office for creating Documents, Spreadsheets, Presentations etc.

My Windows Vista Desktop

My Most used Programs on my Desktop.

Basic Maintenance in Windows

You must carry out some basic maintenance on your computer or you will have problems.

Most computers nowadays come with an anti-virus program. However, many people fail to keep their database of virus definitions updated. All the major anti-virus programs come with an update feature that should be used regularly. Having to update daily is now routine since new malware appears constantly.(Note that anti-virus programs actually protect against a variety of malware, not just viruses.)

You need to have a good Viruses Checker, a good Spyware Cleaner and a good Firewall to keep as many of the nasties from the Internet at bay.

Updating anti-spyware protection

These days, anti-virus programs are insufficient to guard against all malware. Anti-spyware programs are also needed and like anti-virus programs must be updated regularly. Some programs are automatic some are not. If you do not see the Virus Checker and Spyware Cleaner Automatically Updating, right click on the program on the right hand side of the toolbar and update from there.

Preparing for disaster

Unfortunately, hard drive failure is not all that uncommon. If it occurs, everything that is on the drive is lost (unless you resort to an expensive recovery service). Also, if you do get a virus, a lot of your disk may be wiped out. Or, in a variety of other ways, files may be corrupted or lost. Botched software installations, system crashes, or just plain carelessness can lose valuable data. Thus, backups are essential. Ideally, the whole system should be backed up to some external storage device. At a minimum, all files such as passwords, favourite places, address books, financial and tax records, important documents and correspondence (including e-mail), and any other personal data that has more than transitory value should be backed up to some place other than your hard drive. Windows System Restore are not sufficient since they write to the main disk.

There are a variety of strategies for regular backup. An option is to use an external USB drive and one of the imaging programs like Norton Ghost However, since many Computer users will baulk at anything that isn't as simple as possible,

Using System Restore

System Restore does not replace a regular backup procedure but the Windows XP/Vista accessory. System Restore is a valuable tool that can remedy many common problems.

System Restore will restore your System to a previous date, but it wipes out all changes made after the Restore Date, so only should be used as a last resort, or if you have good back ups of all your important data.

Disk Maintenance

Making sure that your hard drives are healthy is an important part of maintenance.

Windows XP does not seem to need defragmenting as often as previous Windows systems but regular maintenance should still include running the system tool Disk Defragmenter.

System Tools

Vista

Start > All Programs > Accessories > System Tools

Diskcleanup

Disk Defragmenter

System Restore

Personally I do not like the windows defragger, and recommend Auslogics Defragger.

File Maintenance

A certain amount of file housekeeping will help your system to be more efficient and stable.

Windows programs use a lot of temporary files, which can accumulate at an alarming rate. In particular, the folders Temporary Internet Files and certain Temp folders can really build up. Keeping these and some other system folders clean is discussed on this page. Making use of the Windows system tool Disk Cleanup is described here.

Disc Cleanup   An easy way to clean out most of the useless data laying around on your hard drive. You will find it in Start->Programs->Accessories->System Tools.

System Tools

Vista

Start > All Programs > Accessories > System Tools

Diskcleanup

Disk Defragmenter

System Restore

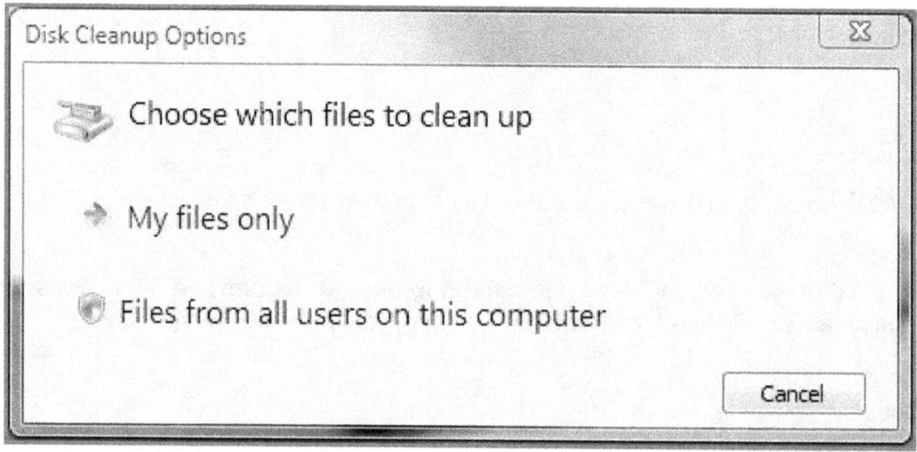

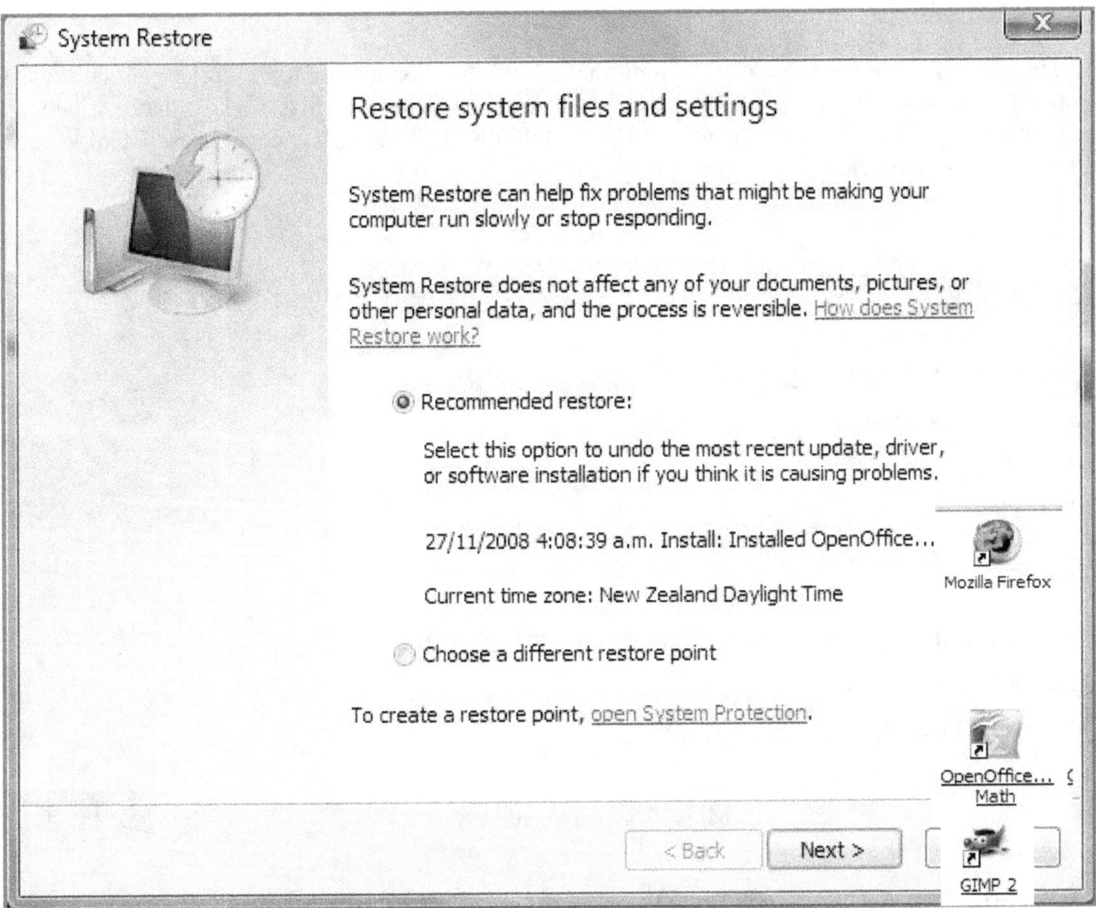

Automatic Windows Updates

1. Click Start, and then click Control Panel.
2. Depending on which Control Panel view you use, Classic or Category, do one of the following:
   1. Click System, and then click the Automatic Updates tab.
   2. Click Performance and Maintenance, click System, and then click the Automatic Updates tab.
3. Click the option that you want. Make sure Automatic Updates is not turned off.

Every Microsoft operating system since DOS back in the dark ages, has contained a tool for repairing corrupted file or folder structures and checking for bad disk sectors. In DOS it was called Chkdsk, in Windows 9X/Me it was called Scandisk, and in Windows XP (and Vista) we are back to the name Chkdsk.

Chkdsk can also serve as an early warning that a hard drive is deteriorating. Disks gradually wear out and sectors may become bad. If Chkdsk starts finding bad sectors, that is a sign that a drive may need replacing. Unfortunately, many hard drive failures are sudden but nonetheless Chkdsk is an important line of defence.

Some Windows Rules

Rule 1 THOUGH SHALL NOT USE (NEVER EVER);

MS Internet Explorer

MS Outlook

MS Outlook Express

Reason Too Many Bugs

Rule 2 THOUGH SHALL USE (ALWAYS AND ALWAYS);

Mozilla Firefox	Internet Browsing
Mozilla Thunderbird	Email
Bittorrent	Music/Video Downloads
Open Office	Text Documents/Spreadsheets/Presentations etc
Gimp	Images/Scanning

Rule 3 THOUGH   SHALL   (AT   LEAST WEEKLY/MONTHLY);

Run Clean Manager

Run Spyware

Run Defragger

As well as keep your virus checker up to date.

Rule 4 THOUGH SHALL (ALWAYS AND ALWAYS);

Use Google Search when you have a problem

Take a Deep Breath and have a Cup of Tea!!!!!!

Ask a techno friend

Email Bill leftfieldnz@yahoo.co.uk

Rule 5 THOUGH SHALL (ALWAYS AND ALWAYS);

HAVE FUN AND GIVE IT A GO, LOL!

Basic Backups, Saving Data

There are some hard and fast rules I am afraid.

You should always regularly save your work to disk. Do save and often. It is no good to go several hours and then loose all your efforts. It is not the Computers problem it is the "Nut behind the Wheel!" I also make different version as I do large projects. Doc1, Doc2 etc.

Next you have to do backups of your data often. Backup to CD/DVD or an external hard drive or pendrive. If your computer dies or is stolen it is too late to cry about it. Do Backups Often!

These things are also part of the previous section about basic maintenance.

Windows Accessories

Windows XP and Vista have many free accessories provided as part of the overall operating system.

From Start > All Programs >Accessories

Calculator

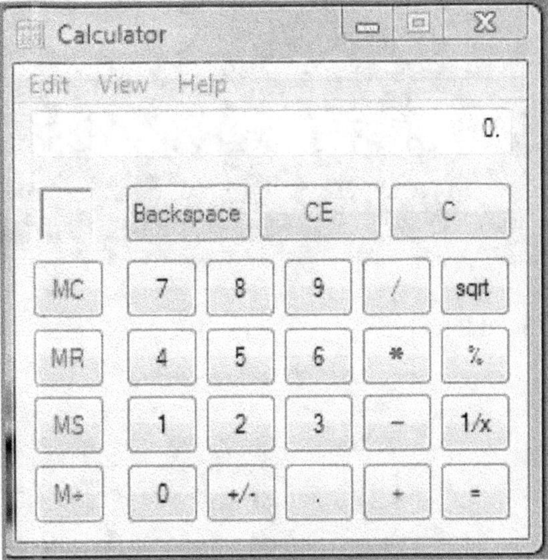

Run

Allows you to run DOS like commands.

cmd

ipconfig /all

Gives you all your network IP Information

Command

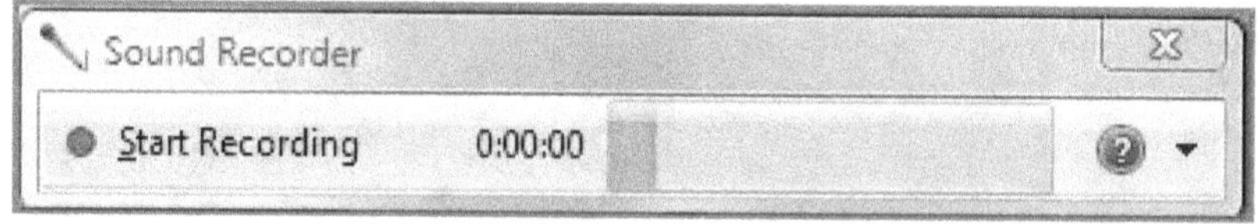

Sound Recorder

Snipping Tool

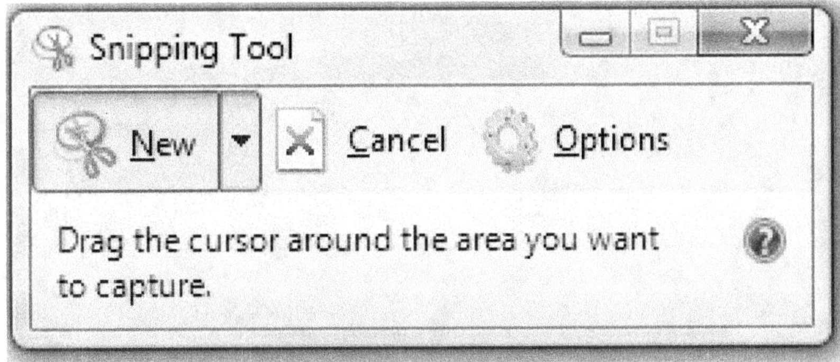

This tool is for Capture a section of the Desktop.

Character Map

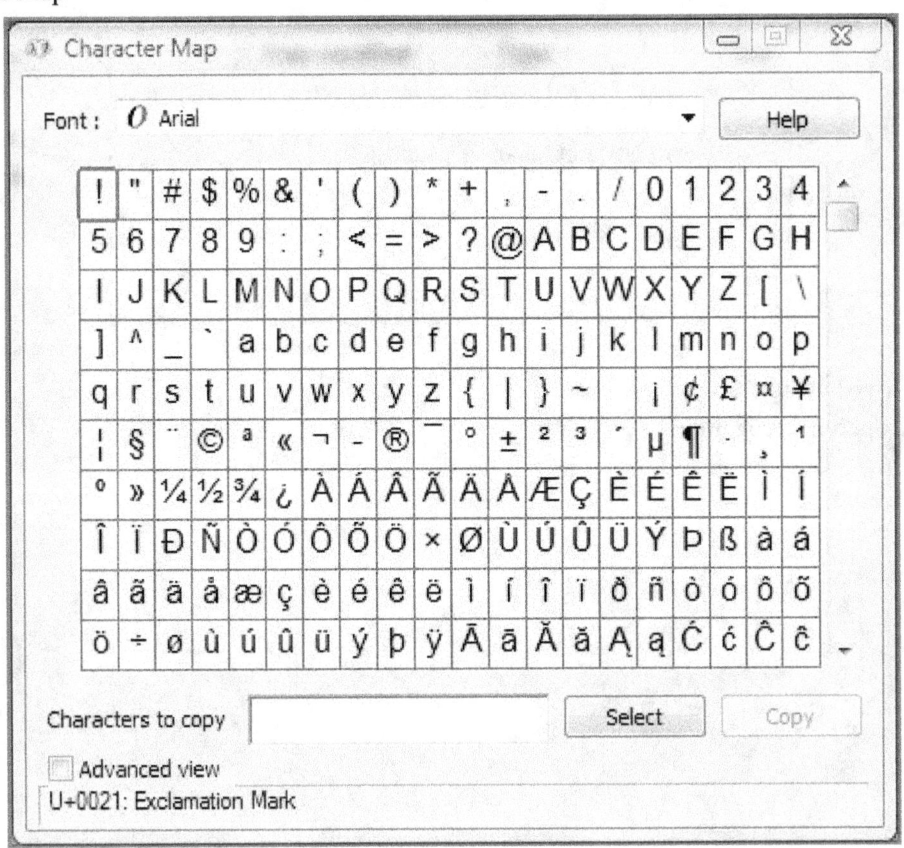

 Some other useful accessories are;

Start

Accessories

Ease of Access

Ease of Access Center

Magnifier

Narrator

On-Screen Keyboard

Windows Speech Recognition

Control Panel

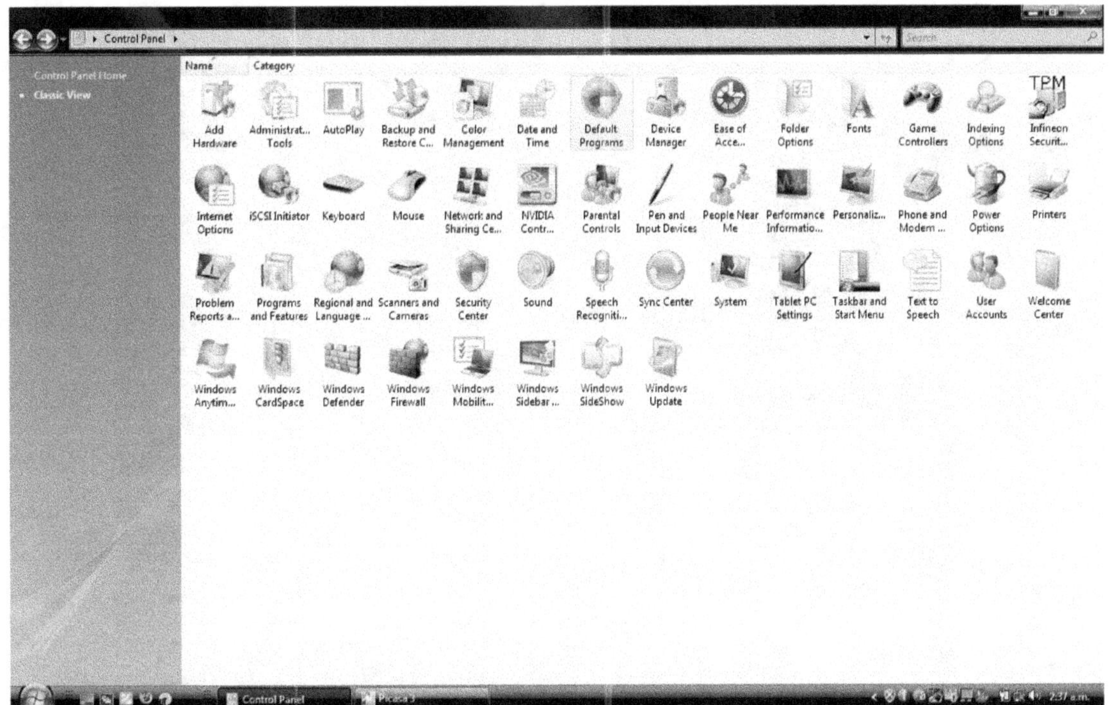

Control Panel allows you to monitor, check and alter many of the hardware, software and settings for Windows and the associated Programs.

Access is from Start > Control Panel > Classic View

Add Hardware is handy if installing new hardware

Device Manager allows you to check what devices are installed and whether they are installed correctly.

Mouse allows you to alter the way the Mouse looks and acts.

Network and Sharing allows you to setup a Network and check your settings

Personalize allows you to alter the Way Windows Looks and Feels and to Change things like the Screensaver and Desktop.

Printers allows you to install or check printers and their settings.

Security Center allows you to Alter and Check your Security Settings.

System allows you to check some Windows Settings and gives some Windows Information.

Windows Firewall allows you to Check the settings for the Windows Firewall

Windows Update allows you to set the settings for Windows Updates and check for any updates.

Device Manager

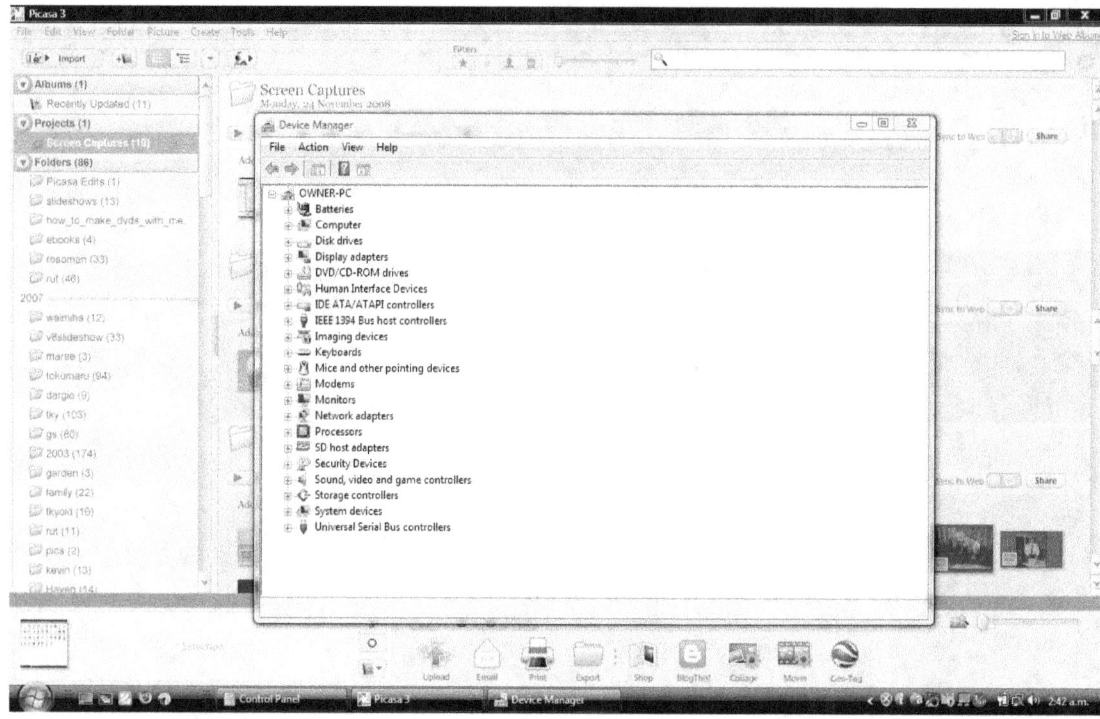

Movie Maker

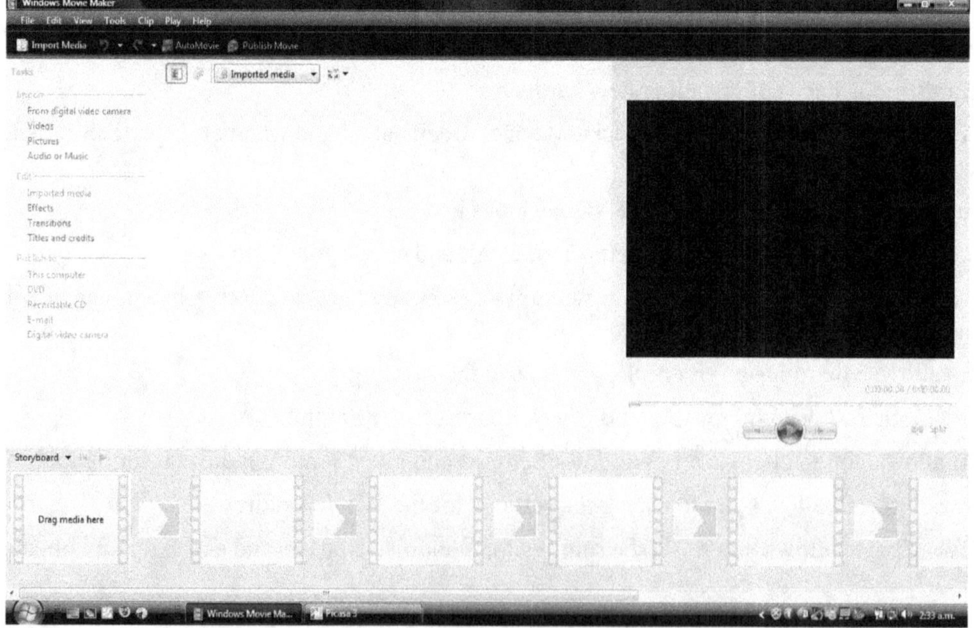

This a Windows Program and does a reasonable job of creating a movie.

We have included other ways of creating DVD elsewhere in this Howto.

Windows Shortcuts

I like to create a Folder on the Desktop called shortcuts and drop in the shortcuts to the various programs I use most often and to the various maintenance tools like the add aware program etc.

To copy them I usually go Start > Programs > Find the Program. Right Click on the Item, Press Copy, the Go to the Shortcut Folder and Paste the Icon. A lot of the Maintenance Programs are under Accessories.

One shortcut I love is to Right Click on the Desktop > New > Shortcut. Type in shutdown -s and Create the Shortcut. Drag and Drop it into the Quick Launch Toolbar (Bottom Left of Desktop). Now with one Click you can Shut the Computer Down.

In Windows ME I downloaded a free copy of shutdown.exe and did similar to above. Shutdown is part of WindowsXP/Vista.

Setup or Install Software

Setup/Install Programs

The Program you wish to Install maybe on Disk, CD, Zip Drive or on your Computers Hard Drive.

First lets make sure the Computer is plugged into the power outlet and the power is switched on at the Wall. **Now Turn on the Computer and Screen. Hopefully we are ready to Rock & Roll.**

If the Program to Install is on CD. It should only be a matter of Inserting the CD In the CD Drive and waiting for the Setup Screen to appear and then Follow the Instructions. If this does not happen, either the CD is not in correctly or is faulty or your computer is not setup to Auto Start CDs or it does not have an Auto Start Feature

If it does not Auto Start, Just click on "My Computer", then You're CD Icon (See Right, it may be called D:) Now you should see a list of files and hopefully one is called setup.exe or Install.exe or something similar. Double Click on the File with the Left Mouse Button and it should start. Follow the Instructions to Install.

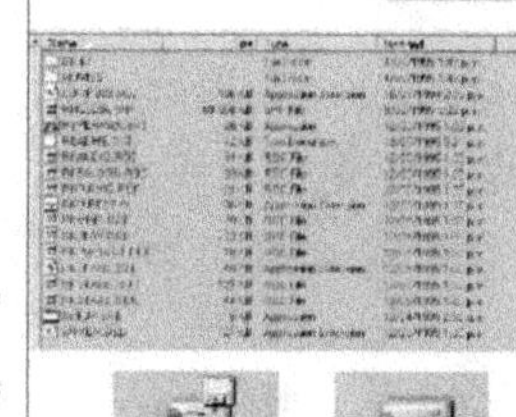

If it is on a Disk, Hard Disk or Zip Drive. Click on "My Computer", then You're A: Drive, or Hard Drive C: D: or Zip Drive Icon. Now you should see a list of Folders and Files, Locate the Folder were the File is and hopefully one is called setup.exe or Install.exe or something similar. *Double Click on the File with the Left Mouse Button and it should start. Follow the Instructions to Install.* **If you see a File called something.zip The File is Compressed and needs to be UnZipped.** Double Click on the File with the Left Mouse Button and it should start. Click "I Agree" if you are Using a Shareware Version of WinZip. You should now see the List of Files. Click on Extract, then specify the Folder were you want to put the Files. Make a Note of the Folder (Say c:\setup) and then Extract the Files. Goto to the Folder by Using My Computer, C: D:, See a List of Folders and Files, Select Setup and then Run Setup.exe Follow the Instructions to Install. If there is no File called Setup.exe or Install.exe or similar, then it may not need installing, just click on the EXE file say FOXMAIL.EXE to Run. To make a Short Cut, Right Click on the EXE File, Select Copy, Goto the Folder or Desktop were You want the Shortcut, Right Click and Press Copy Short Cut to paste and Icon Short Cut. Double Click using the Left Mouse Button to Run the Program. *Above All KEEP CALM and Have FUN NOTHING Will GO WRONG!!*

Mostly it should be a matter of putting in a CD and Double Click on a Program to Install, the same with Downloading Software from the Internet. You need to be little cautious as you never know if the Software is genuine, but I have never really had problems downloading Software.

Also if you are unsure about a particular Software Program do a Google Search (www.google.com) on it and see what that says, it will give you an idea of what the Program is and whether it is safe or not!

For things to work properly in Windows you need some extra software installed.

Flash Player	For Youtube Movies and some things like games
Shockwave	Not used so much nowadays
Java Runtime	For Java Programs
DirectX	May need an update on your system
Codecs	For DVDs, Music and Videos
PDF Reader	Install Foxit Reader

As well as Your Firewall, Virus Checker etc as mentioned elsewhere in this Howto.

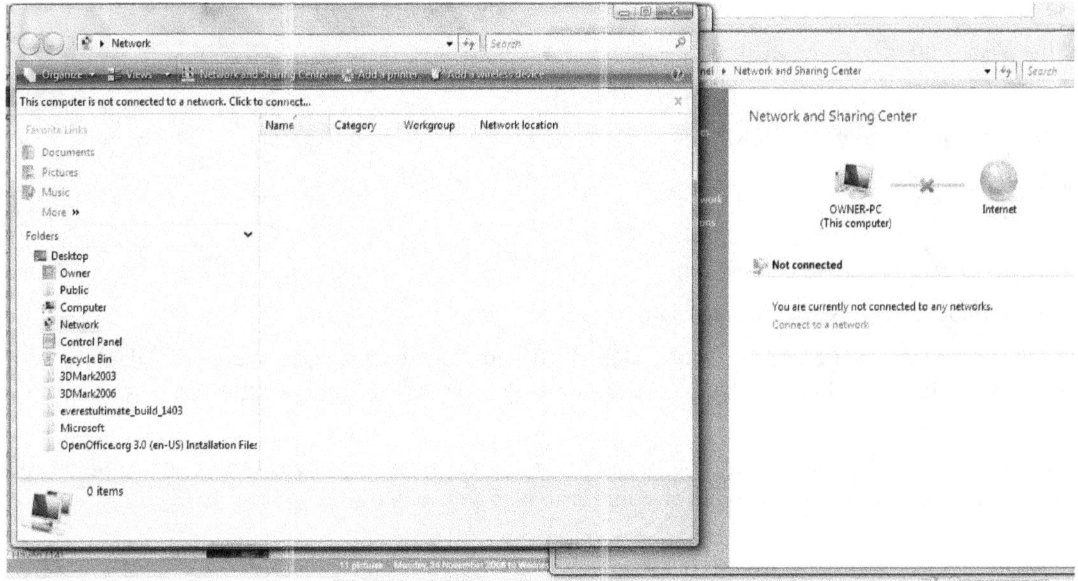

You can either install them or wait till you actually need them, (usually you will prompted you need them) and install them then.

Computer Networks

Make sure you have all the Network Plugs inserted in the right place, it also pays to do it before you turn on the computer.

It should be a matter of;

Going Start > Network

Network and Sharing Centre

Connect to a Network.

You hopefully should see a Network in the List.

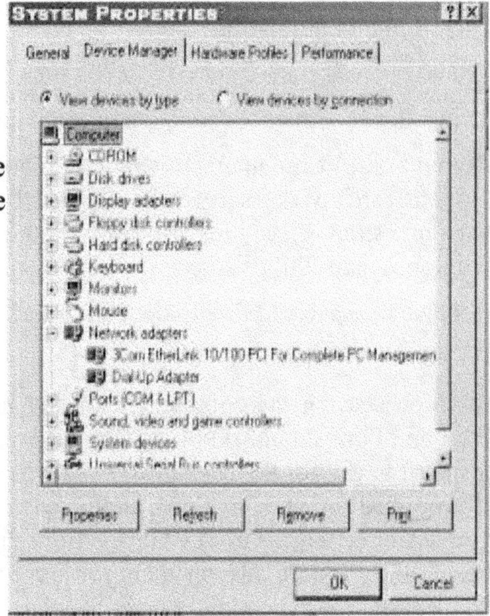

Connect Two Computers Together

For the Vista End follow the Instructions above

Instructions for Windows 95/98/ME

Windows XP is similar!

1) Preliminary

See if your computer has a Network Adapter installed

Left Click on Start, then Settings, Control Panel, System, Device Manager, Network Adapters. You should see probably a Dialup Adapter and a Network Adapter, if there is only one it should be a Network Adapter.

If there is no network adapter then you need to install one. If one is attached to your computer you may need a Disk or CD with a driver for your particular Network Card.

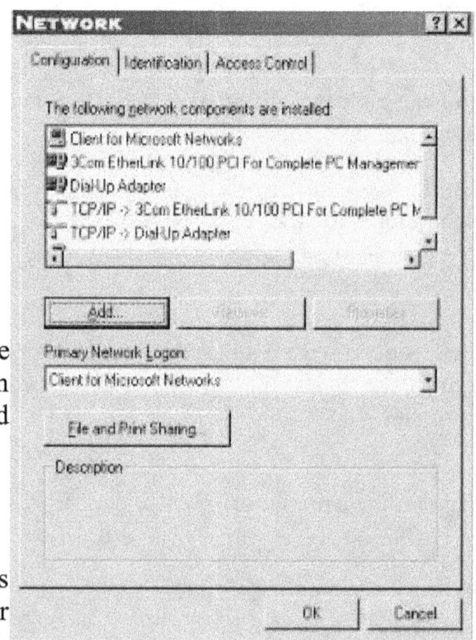

2) Obtain necessary equipment

Screwdrivers

2x NIC 100mbs Network cards (if needed)

Cat 5 Crossover cable

Dick Smith or similar has them

3) Install two Ethernet cards, one in each computer

Remove the Computer Tower Case and install the modem card. Make sure to be earthed by wearing an antistatic strap. Place the card firmly in the slot and hold with one small Philips screw.

Replace the case and fire up the computer.

4) Upon starting the computer with any luck Windows Plug and Pray should find it as new hardware and either install it or ask for the Disk or CD you got with the card. If prompted say you have disk and point the software to the CD or Disk. It should now install and if you use directions as in 1) you can check that it is installed correctly. If there is a red or yellow mark beside the network adapter then you have problems. Try Clicking on the adapter, select Properties and Reinstall Driver and see what happens.

5) After maybe many reboots and mucking around you should now be ready to go.

6) Next we need to setup the computers to talk to each other.

OK One computer has to be the Server or Master and One the Slave; Usually we make the Server the one with the Internet Connection.

On the Master;

a) Left Click on Start, then Settings, Control Panel, System, Performance, File System, Pull Down Menu and Select, Network Server, Then OK, Close, No.

Left Click on Start, then Settings, Control Panel, Network. It should look similar to the Picture Below. But also includes Printer and File Sharing.

If there is more than this like Microsoft Family Logon or IPX then Click on them and then Click on Remove them.

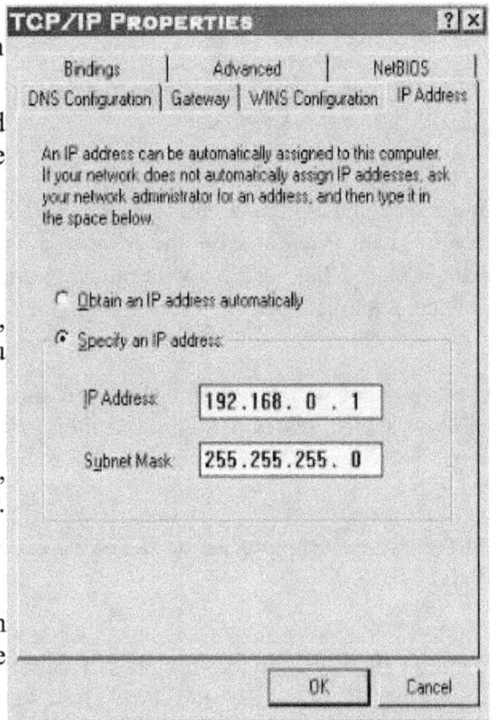

If one of these is missing, Click Add, Client for Microsoft Networks (Under Microsoft), Adapter (for Dial Up Adapter), Protocol for TCP/IP.

If the Network adapter does not appear here then it is not installed correctly. Try some of the things mentioned elsewhere in this article.

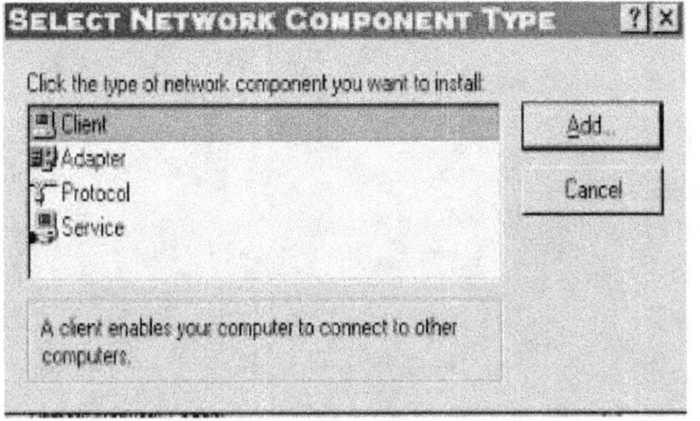

b) On the Configuration Tab if TCP/IP for the adapter is there click on it and Properties. If there is no TCP/IP for the Adapter then you may need to reboot and try again. Under IP Address, Click, Specify IP Address and enter 192.168.0.1 and 255.255.255.0 as Sub Mask.

Click OK

Under Primary Network Logon make sure it is Client Microsoft Networks.

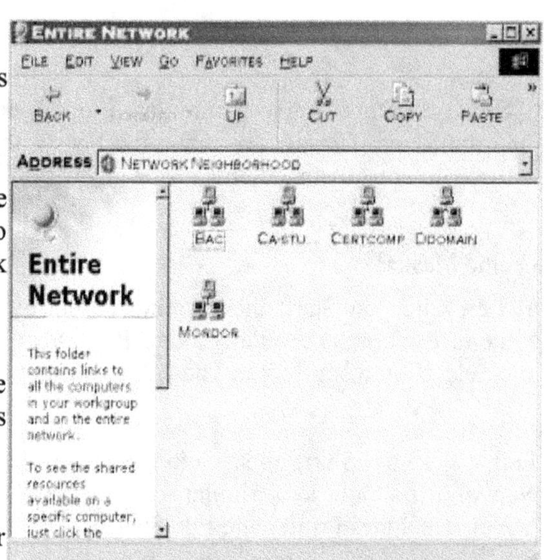

Under File and Printer Sharing, Click I Want to be able to share Files and on the Master, I Want to share Printer. Click OK. Now on the Network Click OK and Yes to Reboot.

The Computer will reboot and then you should see a Logon screen, Enter a Name and then just press Enter.

On the Slave Computer we do the same except for a) and b)

7) Now after the reboot things will start to happen, Hopefully!!!!!! On the desktop click on Network Neighborhood.

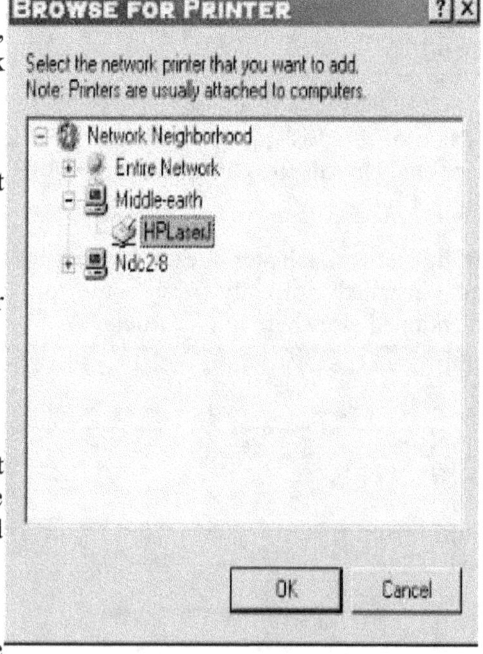

Hopefully you will see something like this, if not do not panic (YET).

Press F5 many times and this may force the Computer to look for another computer on the network.

You may have to Select Entire Network,

And then you should see Your Workgroup. Click on that Icon Twice, If you see two Icons Cool. If you see One Icon (Yours), well that is cool and a start. Press F5 and the other Icon Might Appear!!!

Double Click on a Computer, and then you should see some Folders and then some Files.

If this works then you are up and running!

If Not then you have some problems.

Try rebooting both Computers and see if that changes things

8) To Share a Printer;

From the Master, Select, Start, Settings, Printers, Right Click on the Printer You wish to Share, Select Sharing.

From the Master, Select, Start, Settings, Printers, Add A Printer, Next, Network,. You should see a Computer and upon opening the folder see a Computer.

9) Forgot one thing, you have to actually share something to see it on the network. So on the Computer, Right Click on Start, Select Explore, Left Click on Say C: Drive or the CD D: or E:, Now Right Click and Select Sharing and Share As, You can select the Name, and Access Level you wish. If it is for the kids perhaps they have read-only access so they cannot change things. Or Full if they have full read and write access or by a password.

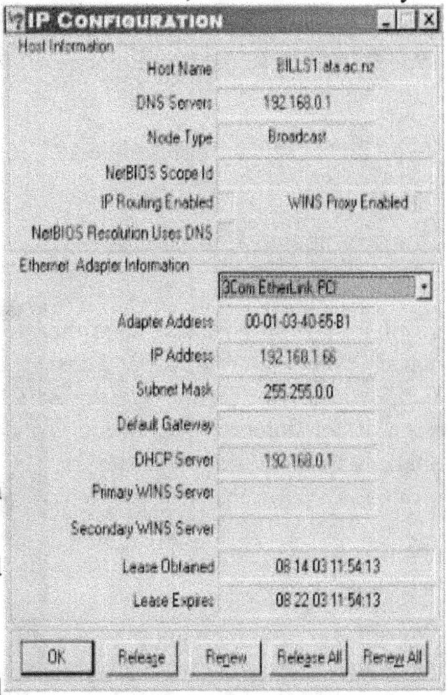

10) Some Links if you get stuck or want more information

www.networktroubleshooting.com

http://www.practicallynetworked.com/sharing/troubleshoot/

http://compnetworking.about.com/cs/troubleshooting/

11) If you are Stuck Try Start, Help, Index, Type in Network and Select network Trouble Shooting and try that.

From the Slave, Try, Start, Run, Type in Command and Press Enter. From the Prompt,

Type in ping 192.168.0.1 and Press Enter. The Router could be something like 10.10.10.1 or something else. Also try www.google.com and see if you get a response.

You should see something like the Pic at Right. (Except I am using a different IP address).

Type Exit to close the Window.

From any Computer, Try, Start, Run, Type in Command and Press Enter. From the Prompt, Type in IPConfig, and Press Enter. You should see something like below. The first Adapter is the dial up Adapter, The Second is the Network Adapter.

Type Exit to close the Window.

```
Microsoft(R) Windows 98
   (C)Copyright Microsoft Corp 1981-1999.

D:\WIN98\Desktop>ping 192.168.1.254

Pinging 192.168.1.254 with 32 bytes of data:

Reply from 192.168.1.254: bytes=32 time<10ms TTL=128
Reply from 192.168.1.254: bytes=32 time<10ms TTL=128
Reply from 192.168.1.254: bytes=32 time<10ms TTL=128
Reply from 192.168.1.254: bytes=32 time<10ms TTL=128

Ping statistics for 192.168.1.254:
    Packets: Sent = 4, Received = 4, Lost = 0 (0% loss),
Approximate round trip times in milli-seconds:
    Minimum = 0ms, Maximum =  0ms, Average =  0ms
```

From any Computer, Try, Start, Run, Type in Command and Press Enter. From the Prompt, Type in Winipcfg, and Press Enter. You should see something like below. Pull Down the Menu and Select the Network Adapter.

Type Exit to close the Window.

If you do not see an address like 192.168.0.? then you have problems.

This does not work on Windows XP

To Share the Internet you need the master Computer running at Least Windows98SE or Better. Windows has ICS Internet Connection Sharing. But that is another story.

```
Microsoft(R) Windows 98
   (C)Copyright Microsoft Corp 1981-1999.

D:\WIN98\Desktop>ipconfig

Windows 98 IP Configuration

0 Ethernet adapter :

        IP Address. . . . . . . . . : 0.0.0.0
        Subnet Mask . . . . . . . . : 0.0.0.0
        Default Gateway . . . . . . :

1 Ethernet adapter :

        IP Address. . . . . . . . . : 192.168.1.66
        Subnet Mask . . . . . . . . : 255.255.0.0
        Default Gateway . . . . . . :
```

Wireless Networks

Nowadays there are many places at home and on the road were you can logon to the Internet via Wireless or WIFI. This especially good for laptops but is great for desktops as well. You eliminate all the wires we used to have to use.

There is also Satellite Options for the Internet.

The first time you use a home WIFI you need to plug it in and setup your router.

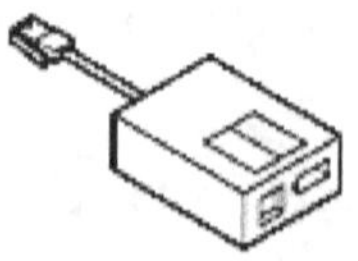

There is one to plug into a power socket and one to plug into a Telephone plug via a Filter that plugs into your Phone Jack.

You need to make sure the Router has a Name and that you institute some Security on the Router.

The following is the setup I have just done for a friends Home Network;

In Firefox log on to

speedtouch.lan

or

192.168.1.254

Your numbers maybe different!

ID

Administrator

Password

1234abcd

Security

On the Router under Home Network > Setup

Add Use WPA-PSK Encryption

WPA-PSK Encryption Key

Enter a Key

Each Computer can logon with WPA-PSK Encryption

Key

1234abcd

Or your Key

WIFI Network

Wireless Access Point - Thomson807AEA

Home > Home Network > Interfaces > WLAN: Thomson807AEA

Details

http://192.168.1.254/cgi/b/_wli_/cfg/?be=0&l0=3&l1=1&name=WLAN:+Thomson807AEA

Logon Details

Help at

www.dslzoneuk.net

www.thinkbroadband.com

Default User Name = Administrator , Password = blank.

Note:-

Some of the above speedtouch routers may well have problems if you try changing the default password and it will appear to lock you out or give you and error message "HTTP/1.0 401 Authorization Required". In actual fact this is an authentication problem within IE7 - try using a different browser to change the password

In Vista, Start > Network and Sharing

Access to Network Connections

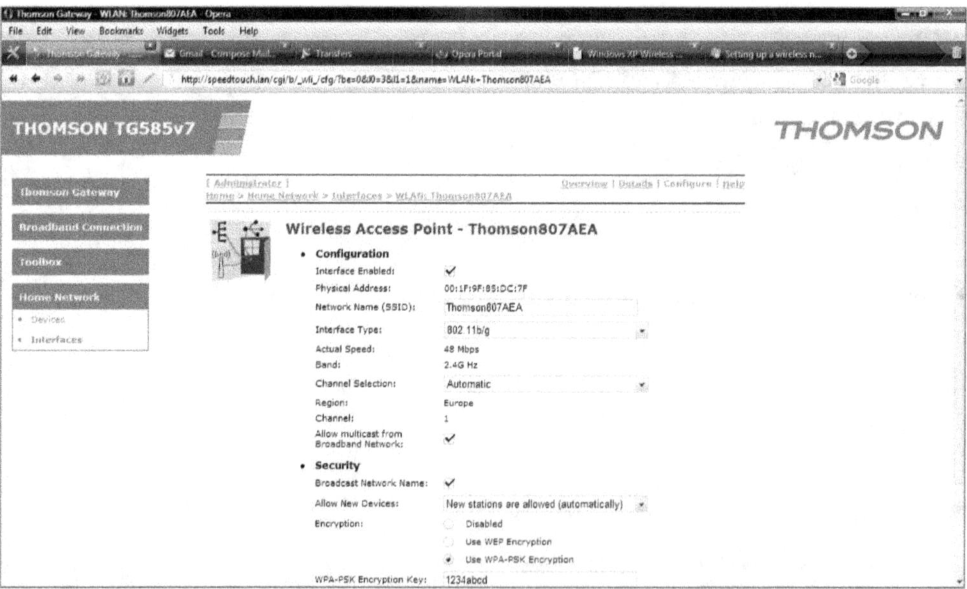

Speed Test

www.speedtest.net

5280kbps   down
718kbps   up

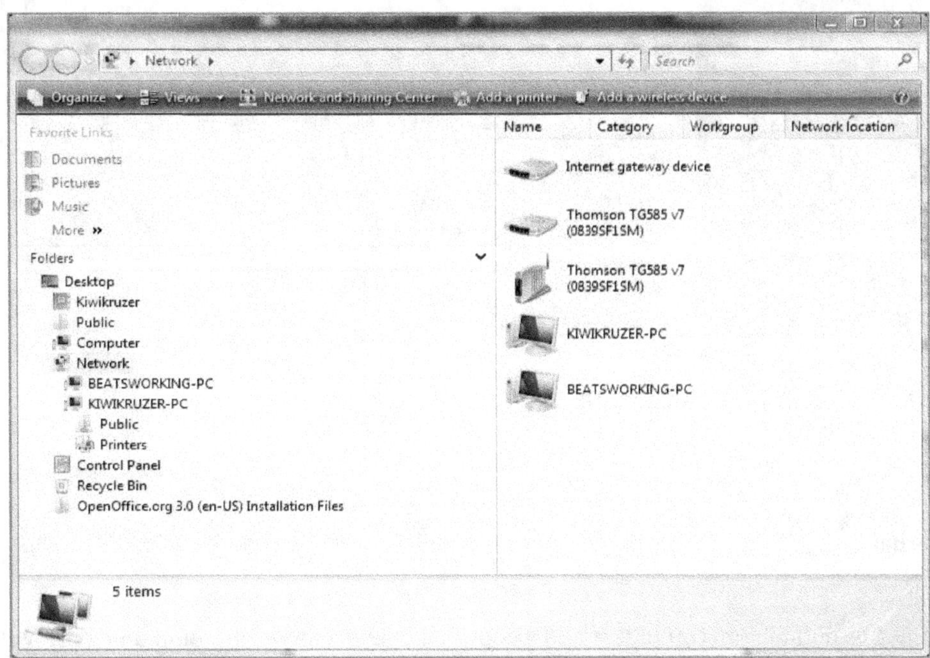

Networks

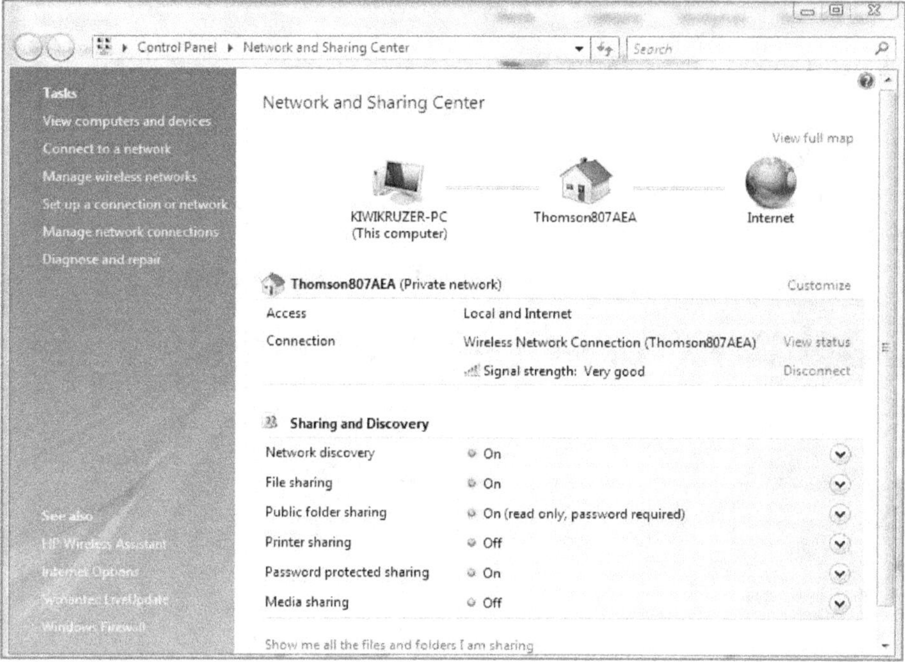

Network and Sharing

The Internet

The Internet is millions of computers and people all round the world communicating with each other.

The word "internet" means linked networks. It is what you get when you link several networks of computers together so that each computer retains its own identity but can still communicate with the others. The Internet is the "network of networks".

You might think of the Internet as being similar to the telephone system. You can ring from Auckland to New York or from Queenstown to Moscow just by picking up the phone and dialling the right number. In the same way, if I am connected to the Internet, I can collect information from a computer in London just as easily as if that computer was in the building next door.

The Internet provides an infrastructure that supports services, some of which are World Wide Web, electronic mail or e-mail, Music, Videos, TV, Radio, Internet Chat or IRC, the news groups, Gopher, FTP, WAIS and Telnet.

To the infrastructure of the Internet, all these services look the same. It is the computers at each end that decode the messages and present them in the appropriate format.

The Internet what can you do ?

Browse the World Wide Web
Partake in the Usenet's
Transfer files to and from your computer
Send and receive Electronic Mail
Listen or watch audio and video
Have a PowWow with the world
Pay your Bills Online 24/7
Shop Till You Drop

Some of the things you can do on the Internet;

Browse the World Wide Web	http://www.si.edu
Partake in the Usenet's (News Groups)	http//groups.google.com
Transfer files to and from your computer	ftp://ftp.paradise.net.nz
Send and Receive Electronic Mail	leftfieldnz@gmail.com
Listen or watch audio and video	http://www.bbc.co.uk/worldservice
Have a PowWow (Chat) with the world	http://chat.yahoo.com
Search for Information	http://www.google.com
Play Games	http://www.pogo.com
Get Lots of Free stuff	http://www.freewarehome.com
Get an education	http://education.yahoo.com
Do Some Research	http://lcweb.loc.gov
Find the Long Lost Family	http://www.familysearch.org

Visit another Country	http://www.swissinfo.org
Find Some Music	http://www.audiofind.com
Watch the News on CNN	http://www.cnn.com
Visit a Museum	http://www.nasm.si.edu
Have a Chat	http://www.talkcity.com
Watch TV	http://www.tvnz.co.nz
Internet Banking	http://www.asbbank.co.nz
Buy a Book	www.amazon.com
View some Pictures	http://picasaweb.google.com/leftfieldnz
View a Video	www.youtube.com
Buy some stuff	www.trademe.co.nz
View a Newspaper	http://www.gisborneherald.co.nz/
Book a Bus	http://www.nakedbus.com/
Visit a Library	http://www.ibiblio.org/
Check the Yellow Pages	http://www.yellowpages.co.nz/
Play Online Games	http://www.iconzarena.co.nz/
Meet a new friend	www.nzdating.com
Find a Telephone Number	www.whitepages.co.nz
Undertake a Training Course	www.webng.com/leftfieldnz/course/index.html

OK I know it is a bit overpowering and confusing. But we have to have some terminology and quirky stuff for things to happen you know!!!

Basically you need a reasonable computer, from $200 to several thousand dollars, a Modem or Router (connects the computer to the phone line). You also need and Internet Service Provider (ISP). And some Software like a Internet Browser and Email Program.

Mostly there is a fee for using the Internet, but there can be free access at some Cyber Cafes or the local Library. (which is were I access the Internet a lot of the time).

Jargon on the Internet

- ✔ **What is The Internet ?**
  The Internet is millions of computers all round the world communicating with each other. Really it is Electronic Freedom. There is hardly anyway to stop you doing anything or

looking at what ever you like.

✔ **What is FTP ?**
File Transfer Protocol, this is the most common way of transferring a file to your computer
Using a browser try ftp://ftp.microsoft.com

✔ **What is Telnet ?**
This is for really dedicated users, as you see a blank screen and have to use UNIX
commands to get around the Internet

✔ **What is the World Wide Web? (Also called the World Wide Wait, as can be real slow)**
The most common way of getting around the Internet. It is a GUI (Graphic User Interface)
using a browser and plenty of pictures.

✔ **What is a URL ?**
Universal Resource Locator.
Usually looks like www.yahoo.com
Goes in the Address Link, just like 7 Whatever Street.

✔ **What is PPP ?**
Point to Point Protocol
The most common dial-up protocol to a service provider. Lets you link your computer
through a modem to a service provider.

✔ **What is a Newsgroup ?**

groups.google.com
These are also called Usenet and is a text based meeting place of minds.
People leave messages and others reply.
Moderated newsgroups are usually about a particular topic and of some use.
Un-moderated newsgroups can get out of hand, people get flamed or bluntly abused.
Great to get feedback on a problem or to seek advice or friends.

✔ **What is IRC ?**

www.irc.org
Internet Radio Chat, one of the hottest and fun things on the Internet.
You can chat all day with audio.
There are three main forums, MIRC, chat.yahoo.com, www.talkcity.com .
You are able to talk, send text, send files and have group audio sessions all online and
nothing to do with the toll bill.
Also you can use Webcams.

✔ **What is TCP/IP ?**
Is the main Internet protocol. It handles the way the whole Internet functions.

✔ **What is HTML ?**
Hypertext Markup Language.
It is the language that the browsers are able to read a page no matter what make of
computer. A universal language.
It is becoming very good allowing people to do some amazing things.
It was invented by a scientist at CERN (Central European Research Network) only a few
years ago.

- ✔ **What are ZIP, GIF, TAR, JPG Files ?**
  Theses are different types of files.
  A ZIP file is a PC based compressed file, you need PKUNZIP.exe or WINZIP to unpack.
  A GIF file is a picture used by browsers.
  A TAR file is a compressed UNIX file, can't be used by a PC.
  A JPG file is another picture file used by WWW browsers, Used by Photographers.

- ✔ **What is Gopher ?**
  These are much the same as a World Wide Web site but have been around a lot longer and are now dying off.

- ✔ **What are Search Engines ?**
  Theses are like the yellow or white pages in the phone book.
  Try www.google.com or www.yahoo.com they are both pretty good!

My Website Front Page.

We strongly recommend that you use Firefox as your Web Browser of Choice.

With Firefox you add many features, like the weather, video down loaders, Gmail Monitor, Twitter Connection etc.

Make sure you install the Add Blocker.

Great if you have Broadband Internet there is virtually nothing you can not do.

I always say the Internet has the good the bad and the ugly, it depends on what you go looking for.

I consider the Internet pretty safe for things like Internet Banking and Buying Online. That is provided you are careful and shop at recognised sites.

Personally I try and use my Pay Pal account as that protects you somewhat from fraudulent use of your Credit Card Details.

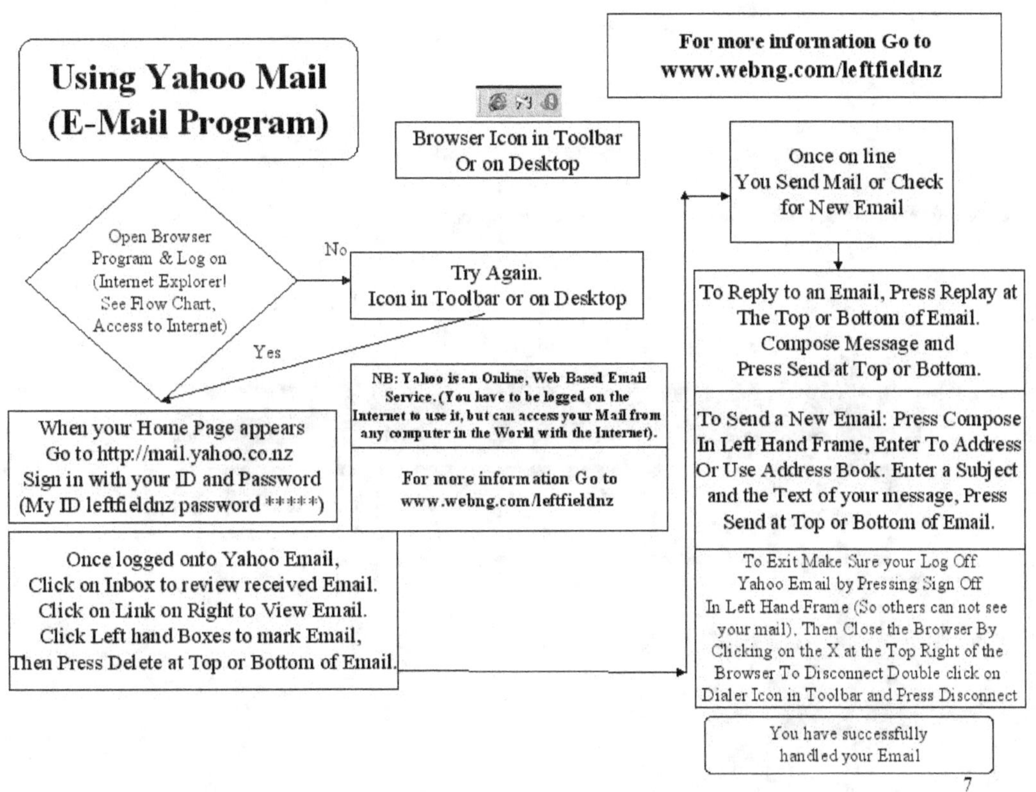

Using Yahoo Mail Online as Web Mail. I also do the same with Gmail.

The Internet is Great !
You can do a Company Search

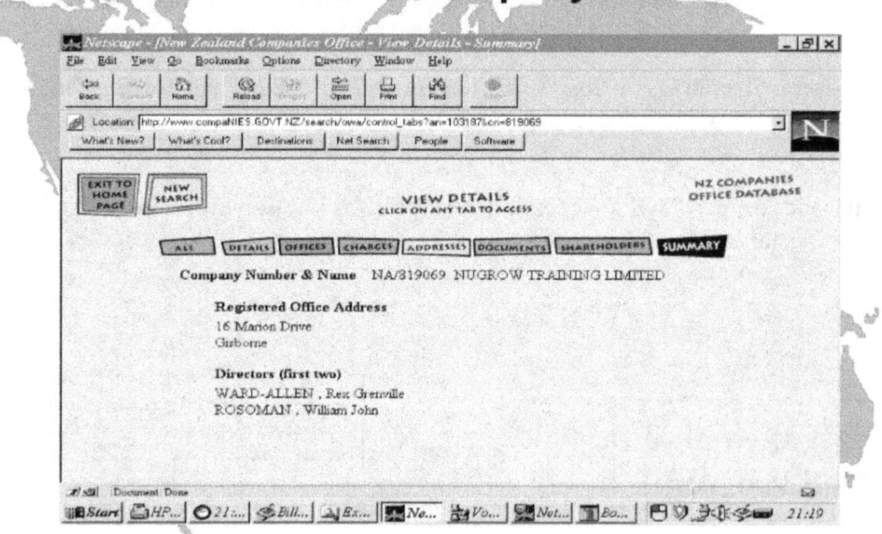

© Copyright Bill Rosoman Dip CS 2001-9 www.webng.com/leftfieldnz

This is a World Wide Web Home Page
http://www.si.edu

© Copyright Bill Rosoman Dip CS 2001-9 www.webng.com/leftfieldnz

Have your Own Home Page
http://www.geocities.com/leftfieldnz

© Copyright Bill Rosoman Dip CS 2001-9 www.webng.com/leftfieldnz

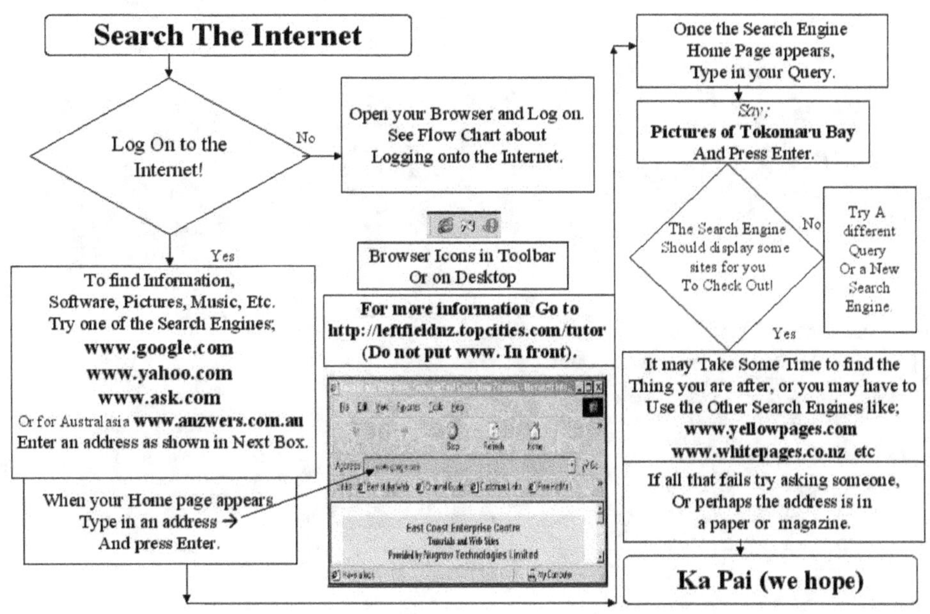

If you need to look for a Folder or File:

(You do not know it's name or location)

From the Desktop Press F3 or Use Start > Search. Or Use Windows Explorer.

Search for all files then enter the file name or part of the name.

You can use wild cards * to assist, like *.doc which contain the word or phrase of "Hamilton" in the file, will look at all the Files with the End DOC for Document Containing the Phrase Hamilton.

You also use ***cd*.*** to find all files with CD in their title or could be ***cd***.txt for all TXT (Text) files with CD in them.

Look in C: or what ever drive and Folder.

Press Start to Begin Search.

When located you can copy/cut and paste as above.

Search and Find Information on Your Computer

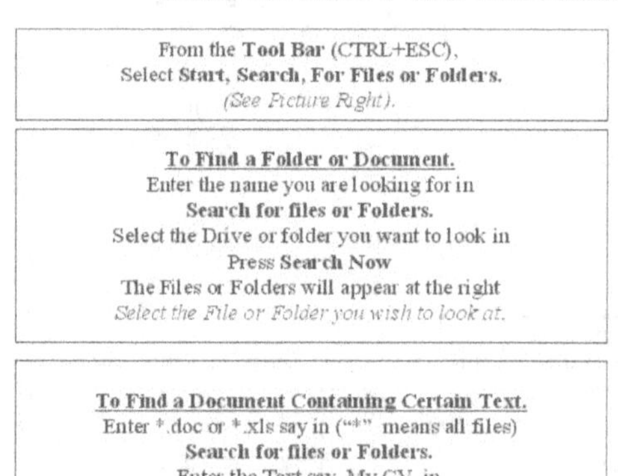

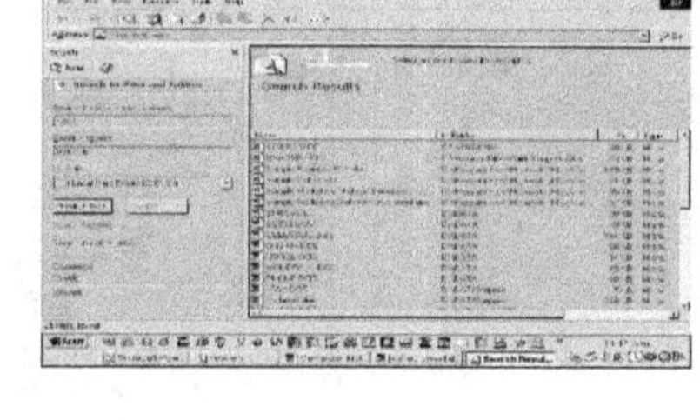

Easy as Pie!!!!!!!!!!!!!!

Firefox to Browse the Internet

Firefox is the Browser on the Internet of Choose. You can add add-ons to enhance the experience, like weather, download Youtube Videos etc.

Make sure you add the add-blocker program.

Look under Tools > Addons > Browse all Addons.

Mozilla Thunderbird for Email

Mozilla Thunderbird is great for doing your email.

You can do Yahoo, Hotmail and say Gmail online using your web browser, known as Web Mail. Thunderbird allows you to download your email to your computer, so you have them available even when not online.

Online or Web Mail

mail.yahoo.com

www.gmail.com

Pidgin Instant Messenger

Pidgin is an excellent program for IM Instant Messengering as it does all the major IM systems like Yahoo IM, MSN IM and Gtalk etc.

You just setup each service, run Pidgin and you are away!

Internet Banking Bill Payment

This is an example of doing Internet Banking.

BTW, personally I have little worry about doing Online Internet Banking as it is pretty safe especially with the proper updated Virus Checker, Firewall and Spyware installed.

Log onto Bank of NZ

www.bnz.co.nz

Click on the Internet Logon and enter your details.

One Off Payment

Click on Transfer and Payments at top of page

Select Make a One Off Payment

Select From Account (Your BNZ Account)

Enter Payee Name and Account Details

Enter/Check Payment Date

Enter Statement Details, From is You Payee is the person you are paying,

Press Next

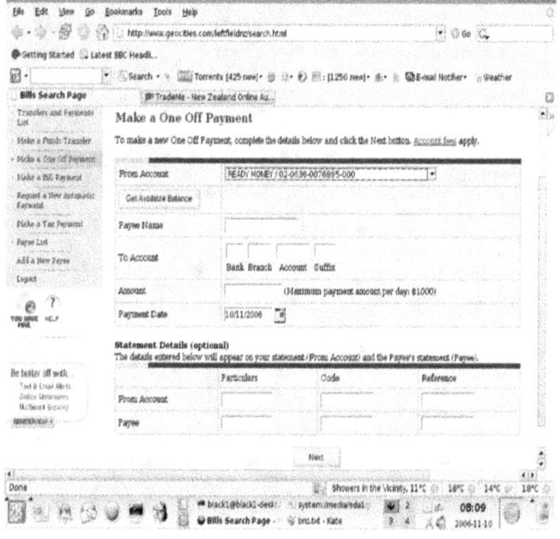

Check Details and Press Confirm

If and Error made Press Back to Correct.

Make a Payment

Click on Transfer and Payments at top of page

Select Make a Payment

Select From Account (Your BNZ Account)

Select Payee or Add New Payee

Enter/Check Payment Date

Enter Statement Details, From is You Payee is the person you are paying,

Press Next

Check Details and Press Confirm

If and Error made Press Back to Correct.

When finished Logout (Top Right)

To make payments online I try to use www.paypal.com as my first choice as you do not need to give out credit card details,

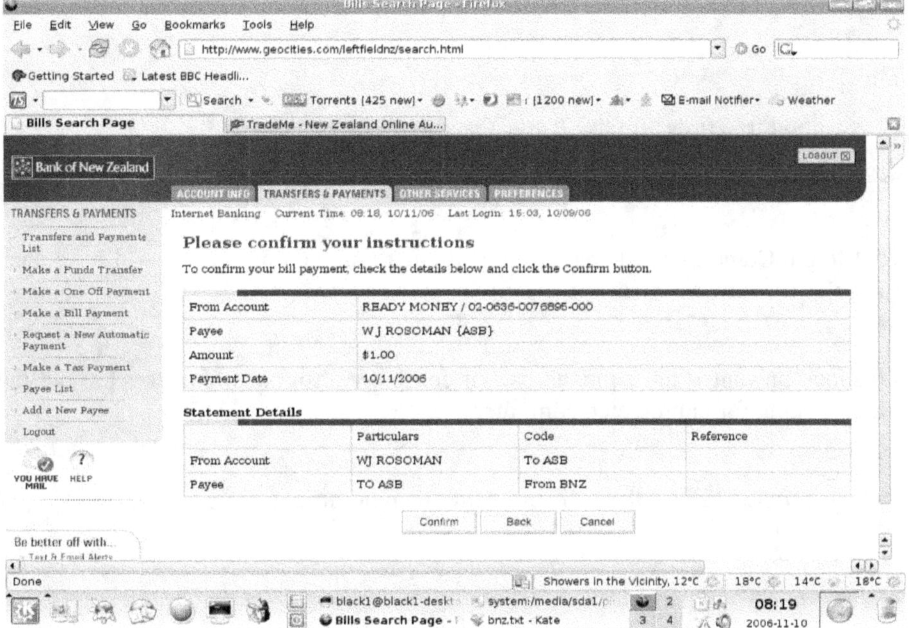

Virus Checker

Avast is a good free virus checker. While it does monitor the computer as you go. It is also a good idea to run it manually as well, say once a month.

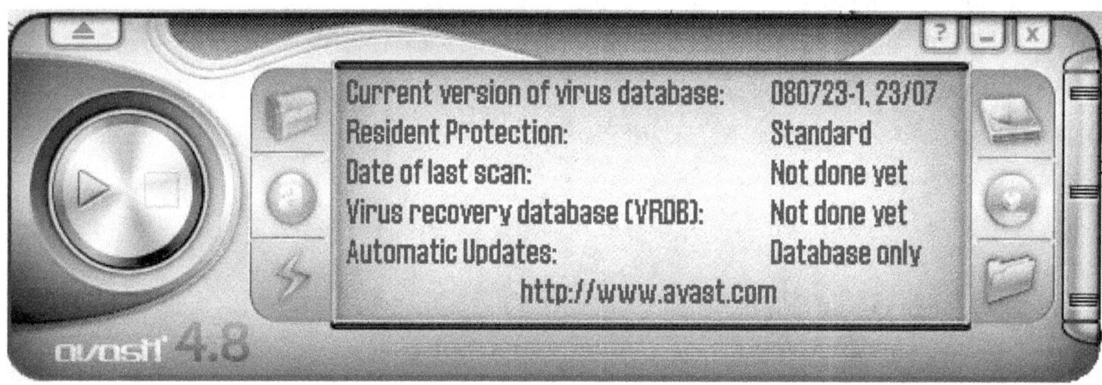

Avast

Right Click on Tool Box Icon

Select Updating > iAVS Update and then Program Update.

BTW You need to register Avast, it is free just needs a registration number.

Firewall

Comodo is a good free firewall for XP and Vista

http://download.comodo.com/cfp/download/setups/CFP_Setup_3.0.14.276_XP_Vista_x64.exe

However I found Comodo was hanging my computer while doing videos, so I have changed to PC-Tools firewall.

Firewalls block unwanted intrusions into your computer. Programs like Bots are out there roaming the Internet looking for unprotected computers.

The Windows provided Firewall is OK but better than nothing.

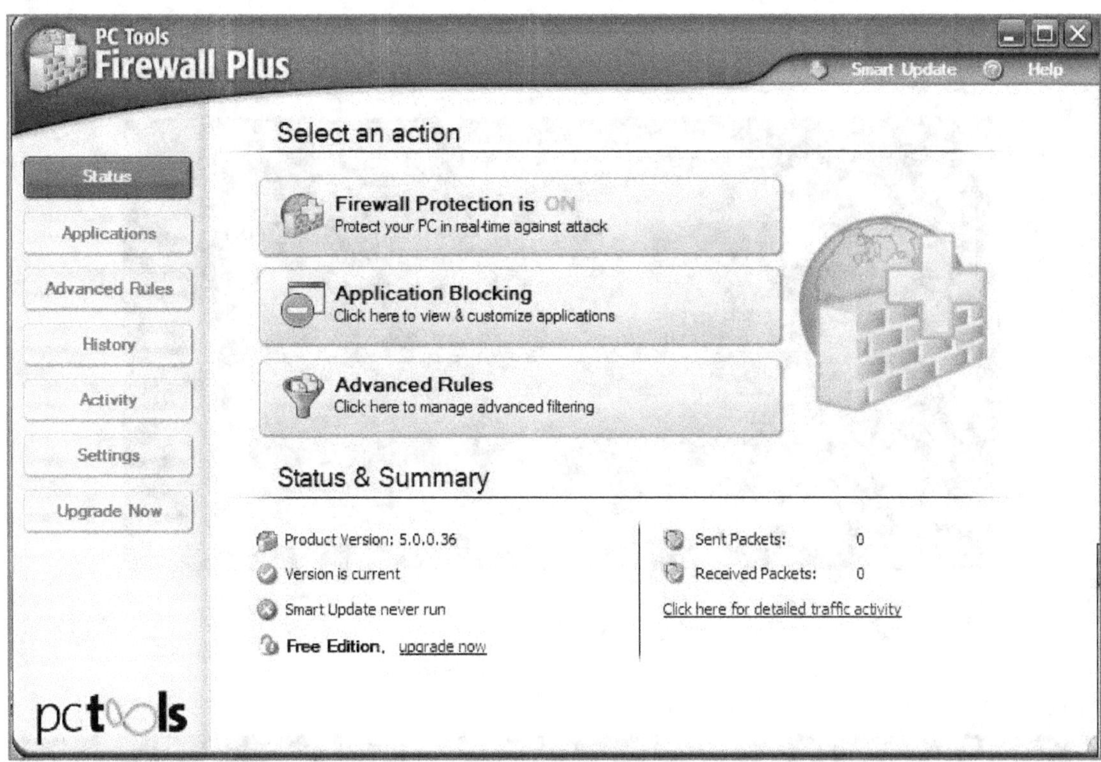

http://www.pctools.com/

Playing Multimedia (Music, Videos)

VLC is an excellent Media Player, for Music, Videos, Streaming Online Radio and Video.

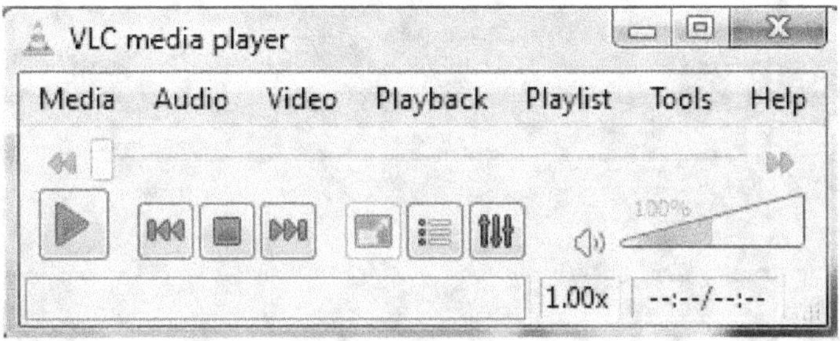

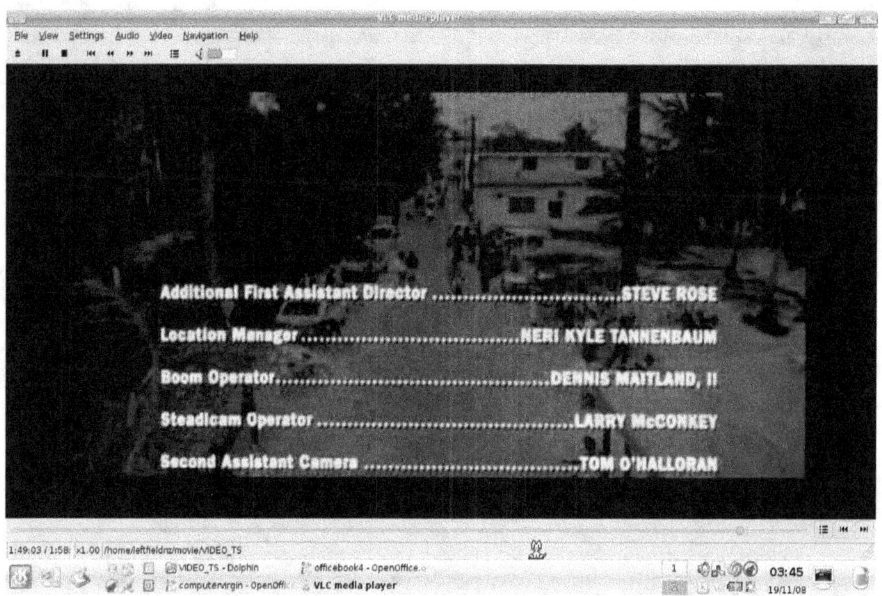

Windows Vista has Windows Media Center

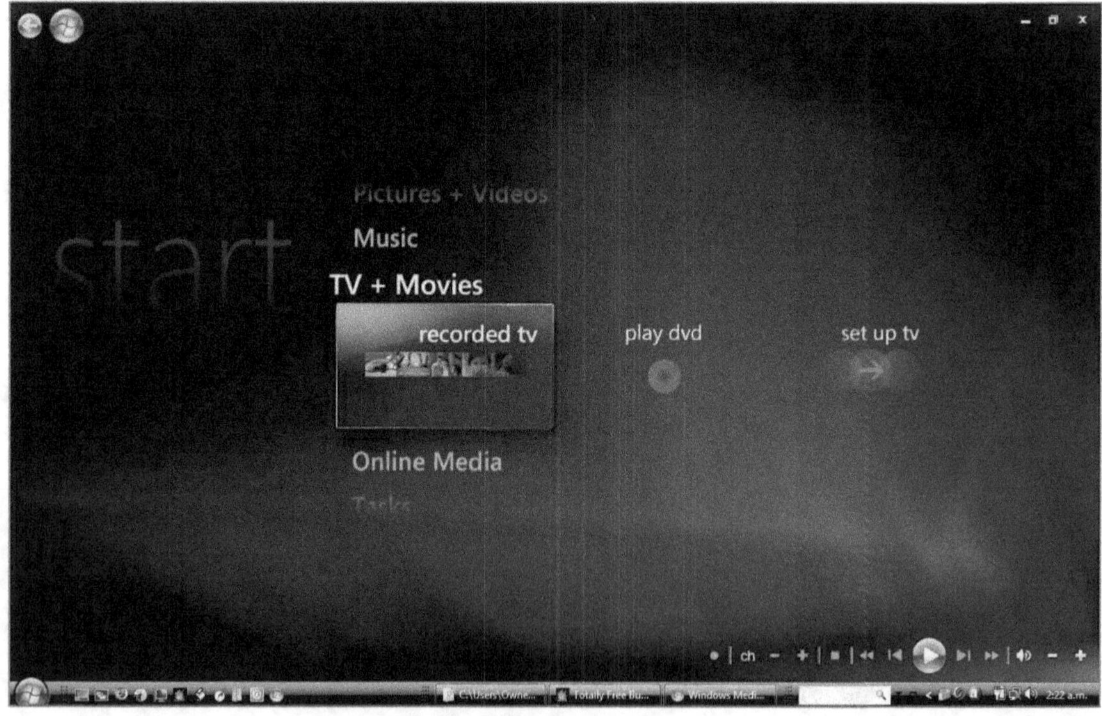

Stream Radio and TV from the Internet

Use VLC Media Player

Media > Open Network Stream > Address > Copy or Type in the URL
http://www.radionz.co.nz/__data/assets/audio_item/0019/8065/national.asx
Press Play

Internet Radio URL

http://www.bbc.co.uk/worldservice/meta/tx/nb/live_infent_au_nb.ram

http://www.abc.net.au/streaming/ra.ram?englishStreamReal

http://www.voanews.com/real/live/newsnow.ram

Internet TV URL

http://www.bbc.co.uk/newsa/n5ctrl/tvseq/n24/nb/rm/video/heads_nb.ram

rtsp://198.116.66.254:554/encoder/live.rm

mms://a764.11292430763.c12924.g.lm.akamaistream.net/D/764/12924/v0001/reflector:30763

mms://skinkers-livestation-client-69bc-bbcworld-
en.wm.llnwd.net/skinkers_livestation_client_69bc_bbcworld_en

www.*cnn*.com/video/live/live.html?*stream*=stream1

BBC Online

Some Streams like the .ram ones may need Real Player to run.

Capture video from your webcam to a file

Connect your Video Source. Via a USB Capture Device.

I was wanting to record VHS tapes to make them into DVD Movies.

The way I found works for me is;

Debut Video Capture Software
This is a nice and free Capture Program and works fine on my Vista laptop.

Setup Options

Select Devices
Video and Audio Devices

Output Format and Destination

Select Device or Screen as your Input

Record a Video
Once Setup start the Video and Hit Record on the Bottom Toolbar

Stop Recording
Hit the Stop Button on the Bottom Toolbar

Take a Snapshot
Hit the Snapshot Button

Screen Capture
You can Capture Screen Shots or Videos of the Screen Activity.

BTW I had to turn off the firewall while recording as it seemed not to like the video capture thing!

Another to try is with VLC

Open VLC

Media > Open capture device

Check "stream output" box

Click settings

Specify a filename (make sure you have write permissions there - usually a file on desktop or home directory is the best bet)

Unselect "dump raw input" (it must remain empty)

Encapsulation method: MPEG1

Video codec: mp1v

Audio codec: mpga

"select all elementary streams" should remain empty.

Press OK

Press OK

Now press PLAY button on VLC.

The video should start recording. You can check this while VLC is recording video by right clicking on the recording file and selecting properties (it will show increasing file size).

Notes:

You can do an HTTP streaming by a similar method you are able to capture to a file.

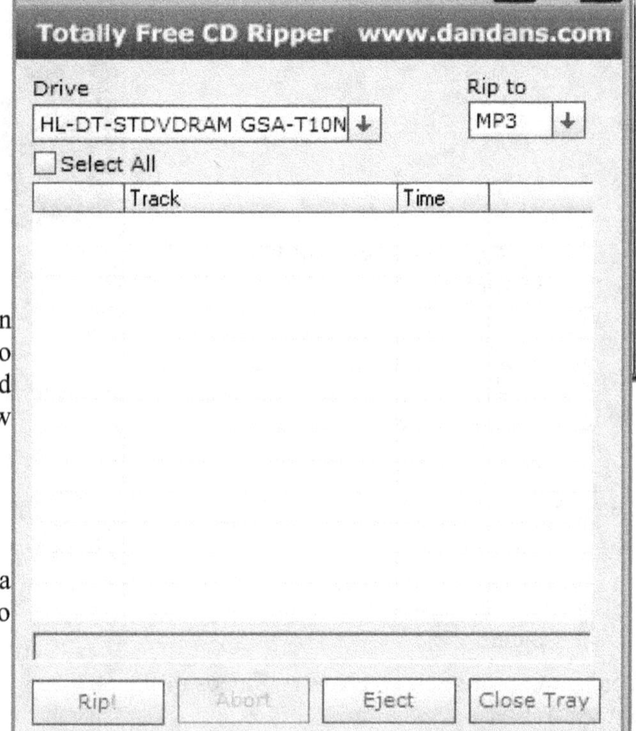

Rip a Music CD

You can use Media Player or perhaps the one below

Totally Free CD Ripper from www.dandans.com

Insert a CD and open CD Ripper, Follow the Prompts and Rip the CD as MP3.

It will take a while but should work fine.

You have to rip a Music CD before you can copy it to another CD or use it on your computer.

MP3 MP4 Player

The Player I have is a no name Chinese
Player. It does mp3 Music, mp4 Movies,
jpg Pictures, txt E-Books, Games, Camera,
etc.

It has a 4gb flash drive and can take a SD flash card.

Seems to be pretty good!

Pictures
are just standard jpg format

Music
 is standard mp3 format

Movies
The Manual said xvid/h263 codec and 320x240 size

I looked at a demo movie on the player it said file properties avi movie and divx codec

I find that this command in ffmpeg works fine;

```
ffmpeg  -i  /media/disk/1/dvd/musicvids/4.mpg  -y  -b  1800  -s  320x240  -vcodec  mpeg4
/media/disk/1/dvd/musicvids/avi/8.avi
```

This converts to avi format and 320x240 screen size.

It seems to me that the size is the important thing.

In windows they provide a converter program. The ffmpeg way is explained elsewhere in this Howto.

Ebooks

Just standard txt files

Camera

The camera is not to bad and takes jpg snapshots, under images/capture.

Games

There are several games on board.

General

Plug into USB with the plug provided and it should appear in Windows Explore..

I find that it is best to upload only a few files at a time and to make sure you safely remove the Player.

It has a main off/on button on the top and a normal off/on on the front panel.

Start is like Enter and Pause, M is for Menu, X is for Exit, A seems to be to record, >|| is fast forward.

The Arrow keys are for volume control and other options.

Great little machine except that after a week the battery only lasts about 10-20 minutes, so much for buying cheap stuff I guess!!

How to Rip DVDs With VLC

How to extract and convert the files from a DVD to mpeg or other formats using the Videolan VLC media player for the use of uploading them to YouTube, for example.

1. Insert the DVD,. Open up VLC and go to File.> Select Open Disc... A dialog box should appear. Go to the Disc tab. Under the field Disc Type, select DVD (not DVD (Menus)). Enter the letter of your DVD-ROM drive in the device name box, and 0 in the title box. Click OK to see if that's what you want to rip.

2. Ripping the Disc. If it is the one you want, select the Open Disc... option from the File menu again. At the bottom of the dialog, there should be an Advanced Options field. Select Stream/Save.

3. Changing settings. Next to the Stream/Save button there should be a Settings button. Click it. Uncheck the Play Locally button if it is already checked (this will stop it playing as it rips). Below this there should be a check box with File next to it. Check this, and in the browse field next to that choose where you want to save the file to. When naming your file, remember to add .mpg to the end, so that it saves as an MPEG video file. Below the File box there should be another box called Transcoding Options. In this select MP1V for Video Codec and MP3 for Audio Codec. Click OK, and then OK again on the next box. VLC will begin ripping the disc to your Hard Drive.

Another program to try to rip a DVD is DVD Shrink. It is good as it will rip and shrink at the same time.

Open Disc > Select the DVD

It will analyse the DVD

Then

> Backup.> Folder

The DVD Rip can take some time, perhaps 20 minutes or more.

Of cause you should respect copyright.

Discovered a trick ripping a DVD. The first rip was still to large for a standard DVD of 4.7gb so I ripped it again from the hard drive files and was now less than 4.7gb and the quality was still good.

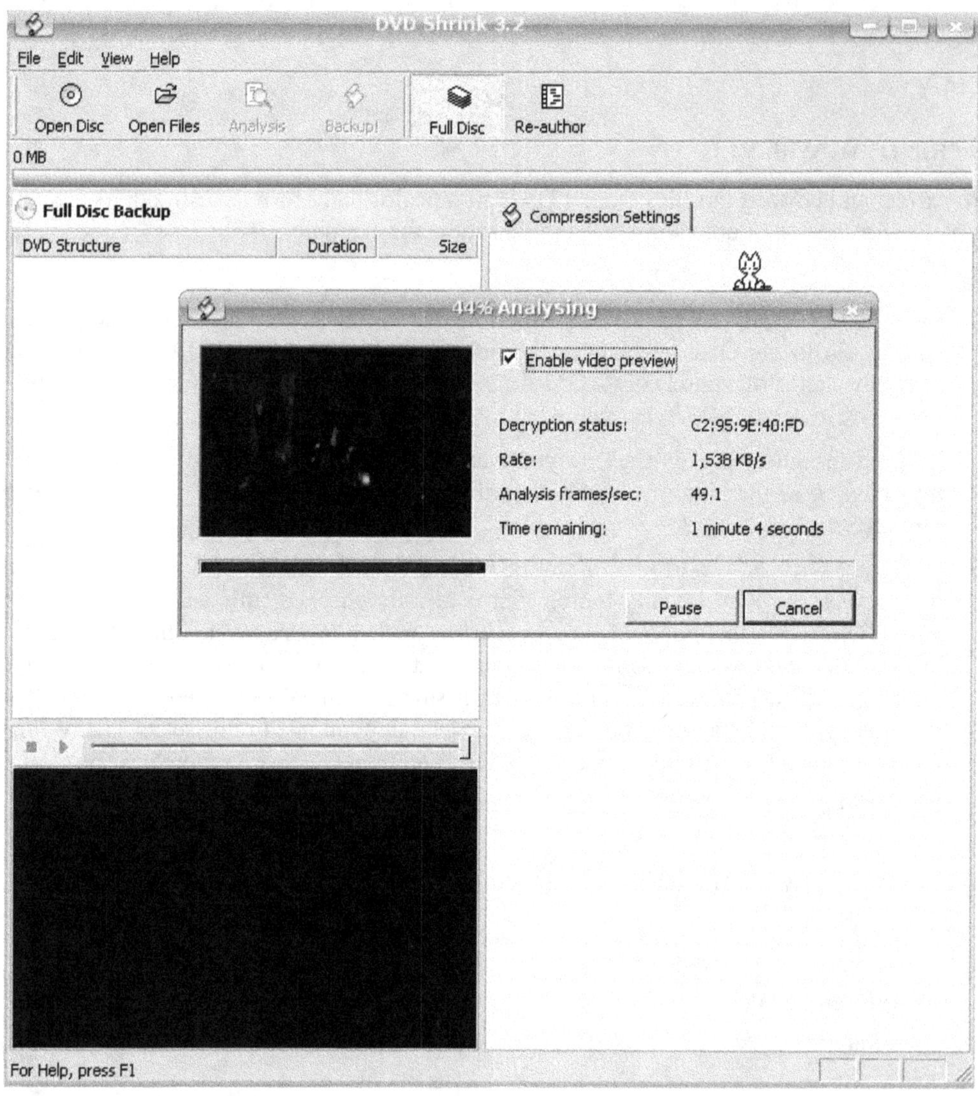

Burn a CD or DVD

infrarecorder is a great little CD/DVD Burner

Insert a Blank CD/DVD in the CDROM Drive.

Open Infrarecorder and Select the Type of Disk you wish to Burn.

File > New Project > Audio CD

In Explorer Pane > Open the Music Folder You Wish

In the Right Pane, Hold Down Shift and Highlight the Songs you wish

Drag to Bottom Window

This will tell you how full the CD will be.

Actions > Burn Compilation to Compact Disk

To Copy a CD

Actions > Copy Disc

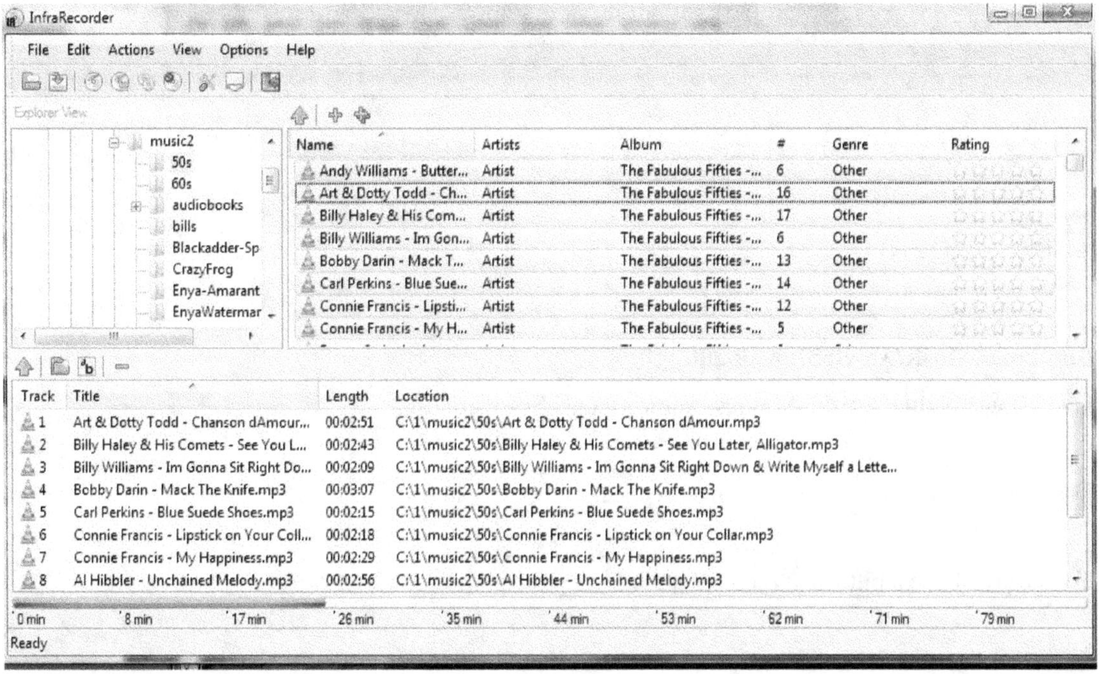

The same approach for other CD/DVD Projects.

I have also found that Totally Free Burner from www.dandans.com is a great little burner as well.

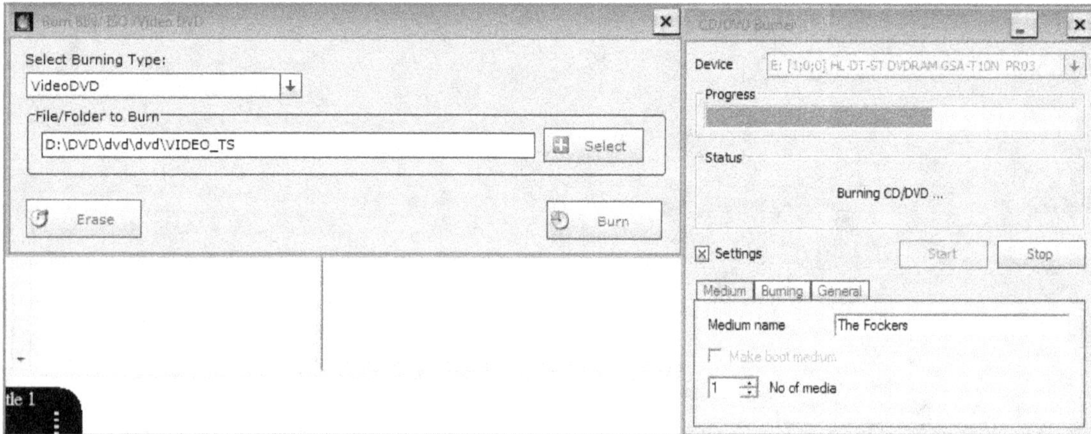

Bittorrent Music/Movie Downloading

Is for Downloading Music, Movies, Audio Books, Software Etc.

Use Google and put Elvis+bittorrent and check out some sites to download the files.

You need to have a bittorrent client installed.

P2P Downloads

Another way to get Movies. Music, Software, Pictures etc is to use something like Limewire Peer 2 Peer File Transfer Program.

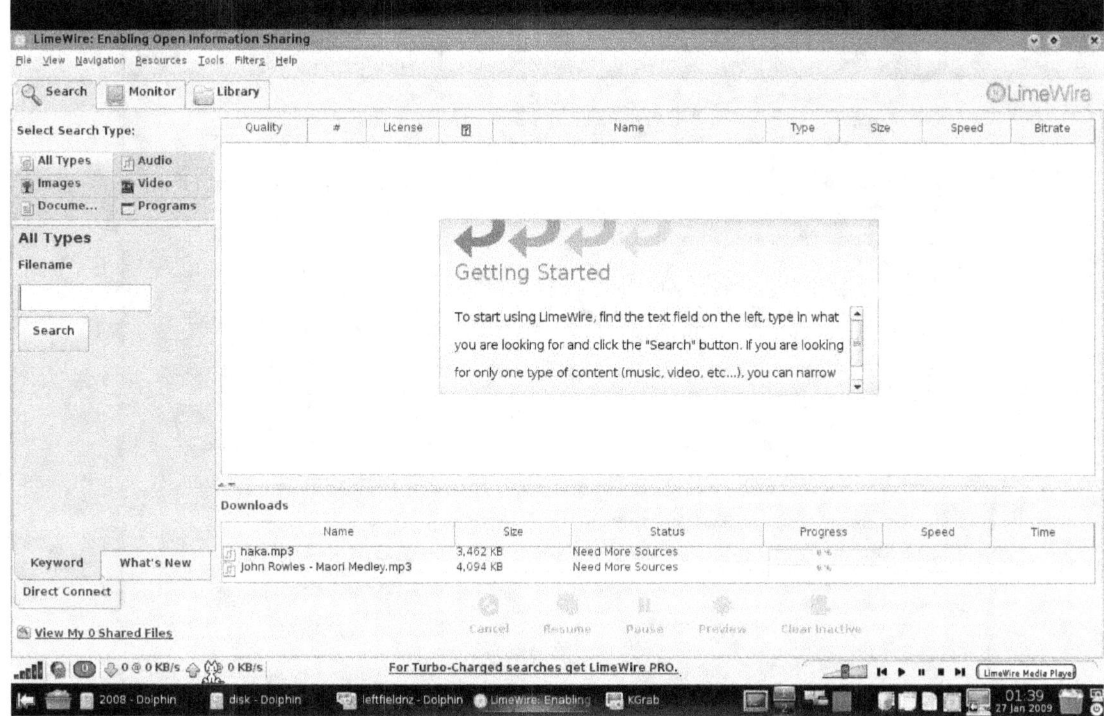

You just Logon and then do a Search, Select the Files you want and Download.

It is not always illegal to use programs like Limewire, for instance if you are searching for Open Source Software.

Defragmenter

Personally I do not like the windows defragger, and recommend Auslogics Defragger. It is an excellent program to defrag the computer. It is much better than the MS program. Use once a month.

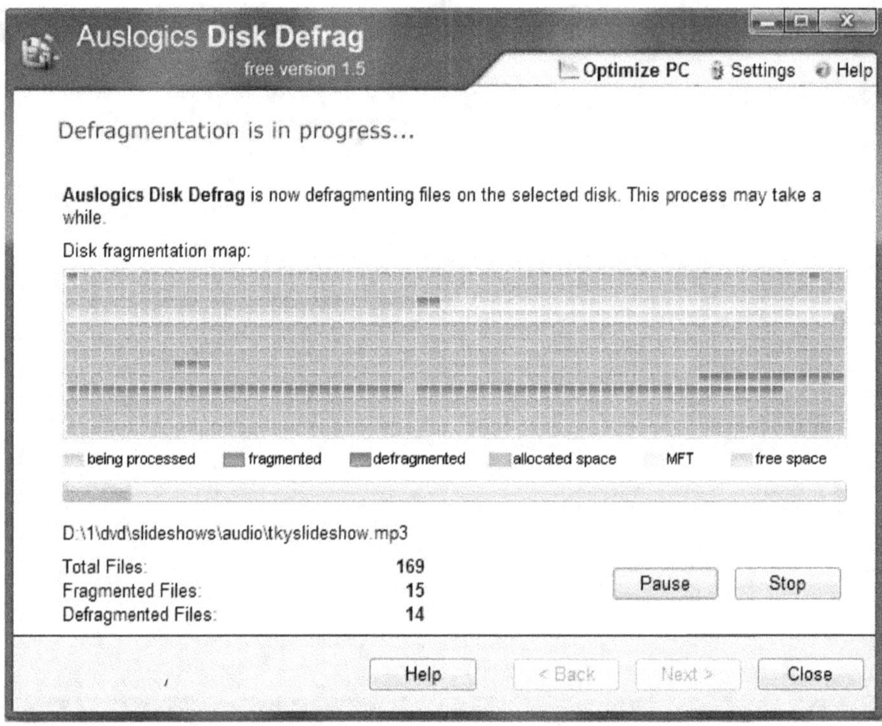

The Gimp Picture/Graphic Manipulation/Edit

The Gimp is great for doing Pictures and Graphics.

BTW When installing The Gimp make sure you install the GTK (Gimp Tool Kit) Program First

To Scan a Picture. Make sure your Scanner is connected to the power and the computer and is turned on. Put the Picture into the Scanner.

Use File > Acquire > Twain or Device > Select your Scanner > Scan the Picture > If you Previewed, Select the Area you wish to scan by pulling down on the handlebars and Scan.

If you have scanned say two pictures at a time you need to cut and paste them.

To Cut and Paste > Select the Rectangle Select Tool (Top left) or Tools > Selection Tools > Rectangle Select. Highlight the area you wish to select using the mouse and click the Left Mouse Button and roll across the picture. Select Edit Copy and then Edit Paste as New Image.

Select File Save as, select a folder to save to, give the picture a name like pic1.jpg (make sure you add .jpg on the end). Select Save > Export > Save.

To Rotate an Image. If the image needs Rotating select > Image Transform and Rotate 90 or 180 degrees. Or use Tools > Transform Tools > Rotate.

To Resize an Image. You will see the size of the image at the top of the toolbar. To resize select > Image > Scale Image > for the Width Select say 900 pixels > Press TAB > Select Scale. If that is ok Select File Save. (This Size would be suitable to email or upload to a website).

You can also add text etc.

You can also use OCR, Optical Character Recognition (Copy Text).

To Crop a Pic

Of course if you crop the pic just to include the actually bits you want and this will reduce it further.

Use Gimp, and the "Select rectangular Regions" Tool, if the Toolbox is not visible go to Tools > Toolbox.

Select the part of a Pic you want > Press CTRL+C to Copy > Press Edit > Paste as New >

We can sharpen the pic, change the brightness and contrast and crop easily.

To Email a Pic

Have you considered say using http://briefcase.yahoo.com or perhaps http://picasaweb.google.com and storing it online in your briefcase and tell your friends were the link is. It saves filling up peoples in boxes. Also try www.esnips.com for large files.

Personally I get several hundred emails a week and the less time I spend waiting for things to download the better. At the moment I am receiving several emails a day with the latest virus doing the rounds, as well as all the other junk mail I get.

You can also compress the photo Right Click on file or files, Select Action, Compress, Select Compress as File.zip, though it probably will not compress the file much more.

Go to your Email Program, Compose a New message then

press the PaperClip, Locate the File in the Folder were you saved it and then attach and send the file.

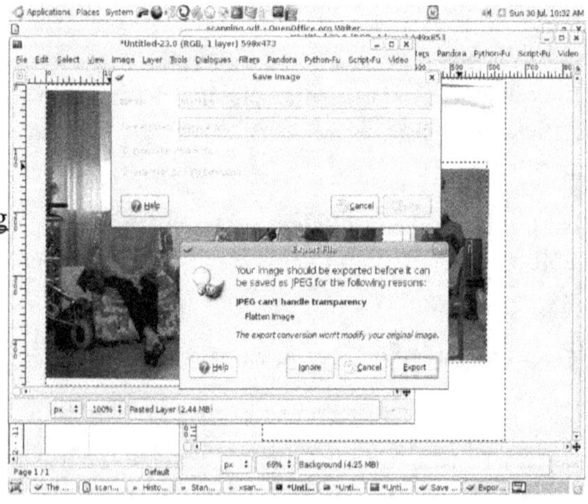

Another way so all your friends will not get clogged up emails and still be talking to you, is to send through ICQ, Yahoo Messenger for instance.

Have Fun1!!!!!!!!!!!!!!!!!!!!!!!!!!!!!!!!

Scanning/Manipulating Pictures

Use The Gimp for Scanning and Manipulating Images.

Applications > Graphics > Gimp Image Editor

Turn on the Scanner!

From The Gimp

File > Acquire > Twain or Xsane > Device Dialog

Put Item to be scanned into scanner.

Press Scan and wait for Scanner to complete its task.

You can adjust Brightness, whether Colour or Black and White Etc Before Scanning.

<u>To Cut out a part of the Scan</u>
Tools > Selection Tools > Rect Set
Locate Corner you wish to cut out, hold down left mouse and move mouse to other point to cut
Select
Edit Copy > Edit paste as New >save Image (as below)

Save Image
File > Save As > Filename.jpg > Select Folder (Browse for Other Folders) > Save > Export (if asked) > OK

<u>Scale Image</u>
Image > Scale Image > Enter New Width > Press TAB

Image will scale to new size.
Save as above.

<u>Using Images</u>
It is better to open Open Office Writer or better still Open Office Impress and import the picture
Insert > Picture > From File > Locate Folder and File and Import.
Right click on picture and change Wrap to Optimal Wrap
Use Corner handles to resize image
Hold Left Mouse Button down to relocate Image.
File Print to Print Out

Rotate Image
Tools > Transform Tools > Rotate
Enter Angle + or – and Rotate

You can also use OCR, Optical Character Recognition (Copy Text) by using Kmenu > Graphics >

Xsane.

Pictures in Picasa

Use Picasa to view and organise your pictures. Picasa does some wonderful things.

Run Picasa and wait for it to catalogue all the pictures on your hard drive. (Slow the first time you do it).

Under Create

set as desktop

Make a Poster

Picture collage

Screensaver

Make a Movie

Publish to Blogger

Picasa will also make a great CD of Photos and upload them to picasa.

You can also run a slideshow from Picasa.

In Picasa

Locate the Pictures you wish to put onto CD

Search for House say!

Select > Folder > Create a Gift CD

Click Add More

Select the Folder Containing the Pictures or Click on individual Pictures.

Select Burn Disc

When Finished

Locate the ISO Image

Insert a Blank CDR

Right Click and Open CD Burner and Burn the Image.

You have a nice CD with Pictures and a nice program (Windows) PicasaCD.exe Click on this and then Click on the Main Picture, A Slideshow will start, which you can slow down or speed up.
Press ESC and Exit to Close

Will also play on most DVD Players.

To Upload to the Internet.
Open Picasa
Locate Pictures
Click on Web Album
Log into Picasa
Select Folder or Photos and Upload.

Easy as Pie

Creating a Panorama

There are several panorama programs.

One is Pandora which is an add-on for the Gimp.

You select a batch of photos and create a panorama of them.

Sound and Audio

Audacity is a great little Audio Program.

You can record sound, cut and paste sound and join different sounds like a voice introduction and then some music.

I use the voice then music option when making video slideshows of still pictures.

You can also convert files from one format to another with Audacity.

Use > File > Export

Bluetooth from Cellphone

You can transfer information and pictures from your cellphone using Bluetooth etc.

Click on Bluetooth Icon on Toolbar

Click Add

Then Click > My Device is Ready

Click Next

When Bluetooth Item Appears, Click on it and Then Next.

Enter a Password

Should now be Connected

Do the same password on your cellphone and you are away!

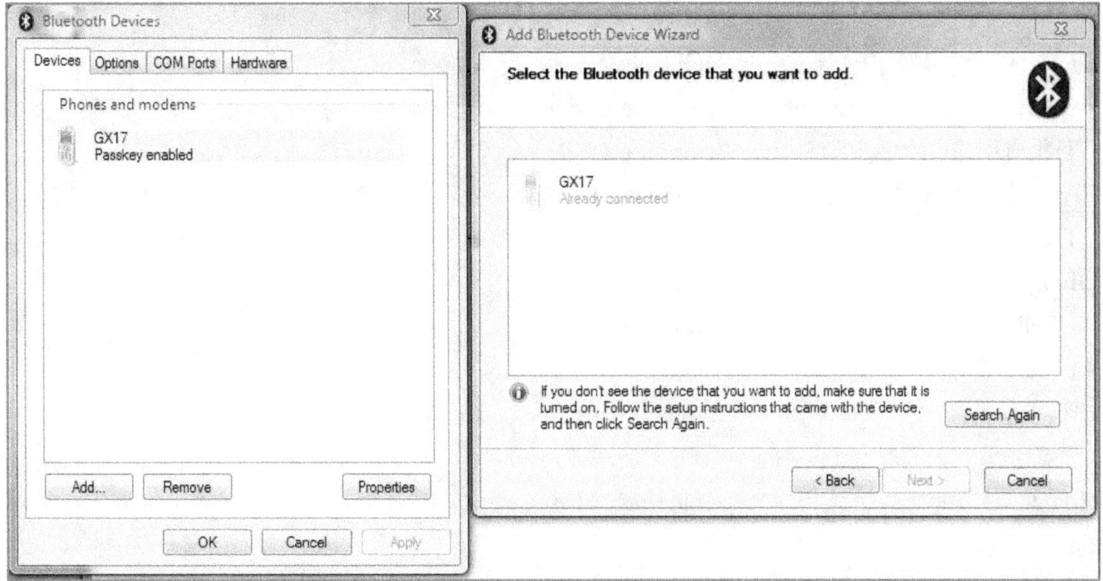

Basic Windows Commands

To make things a lot quicker using various Windows Programs is easy using a few of the Shortcut Keys,

CTRL+C	Copy
CTRL+V	Paste
CTRL+X	Cut
CTRL+P	Print
CTRL+S	Save
CTRL+O	Open
CTRL+B	Bold
CTRL+U	Underline

CTRL+N	New File
CTRL+E	Center
CTRL+A	Select All
CTRL+R	Replace
F5	Reload/refresh or Go to a Page
F2	Rename
F3 or CTRL+F	Find
F7	Spell Check
HOME	Beginning of line
CTRL+HOME	Beginning of file
END	End of Line
CTRL+END	End of File
DEL	Delete
ALT+F4	Exit Program
ALT+F1	Menu
F12	Bullets
Home	Beginning of Row
End	End of Row
Ctrl+Home	Beginning of File
Ctrl+End	End of File
Del	Delete Highlighted
Insert	Toggle between Insert and Over type
Page Up	Up One Screen
Page Down	Down One Screen
Caps Lock	Capitals
Shift+Key	Capital or alternative Key

These are the Basic Command Short Cuts, of Cause you can go File > Save with you mouse but the Keyboard Short Cuts are so much easier and better on the hands.

Suggested Websites

Email via Website	www.gmail.com

Web search	www.google.com
Spyware Cleaner	www.lavasoft.com/products/ad_aware_free.php
Internet Hotspots	www.telecom.co.nz/wifi
Bill's Email	leftfieldnz@gmail.com
Bill's Web Site	www.webng.com/leftfieldnz
Google Linux	www.google.com/linux
Picasa Picture Viewer	http://picasa.google.com
Pidgin Instant Messenger	www.pidgin.im
Ubuntu	http://ubuntuguide.org
Linux Novice	http://www.linuxnovice.org/
Trade Me	http://www.trademe.co.nz/
Bittorrent Client	www.bittorrent.com
Flash Earth	http://www.flashearth.com/
Multimedia Player VLC	www.videolan.org
Virus Checker	http://www.avast.com/eng/download-avast-home.html
Firefox Web Browser	http://www.mozilla.com/en-US/firefox/
Defragmenter	http://www.auslogics.com/en/software/disk-defrag/download
Open Office	www.openoffice.org
Jalbum Picture Album Maker	www.jalbum.net
Thunderbird Email	http://www.mozilla.com/en-US/thunderbird/
The Gimp for Graphics/Photos	www.gimp.org
Firewall	http://download.comodo.com/cfp/download/setups/CFP_Setup_3.0.14.276_XP_Vista_x64.exe
CD Ripper/DVD Burner	www.dandans.com

Wireless Hotspots

Connect your Computer to the Wifi Hotspot, usually click on the Network Icon on the Bottom Right of the Toolbar, it should say a Network is Available. Click on that and then Connect.

Then open a Browser like Firefox and click Home to log onto a page like the Telecom Hotspot below.

You need to click on one of the three options to gain access to the Internet.

Once that is completed you should be able to carry as normal.

This a the Telecom Hotspot at McDonald's Frankton, Hamilton on SH1.

I can log onto this site sitting in my Camper van parked Outside McDonald's.

Once connected you can do the usual Internet things like Email Web Browsing etc. Mind you at the price you would not want to spend too long online.

The best thing is to logon and check your email. Then logoff and compose a reply, log back on to send the replies. This is the same whether your are using an Email Client on your PC like Thunderbird, or are using a Web based Email system like Gmail or Yahoo or Hotmail. Just select (CTRL+A) copy (CTRL+C) and paste (CTRL+P) to a text editor.

Now I mostly use one of the local libraries for free access via wifi. I can do a lot of things but not bittorrent, Skype or any pornography etc, but that is ok.

USB Devices/Cameras

For USB Storage devices just plug them in and they should appear on the desktop.

Make sure when you want to disconnect the device, make sure you right click on the icon and click on Safely Remove Device.

For Cameras either plug the camera in the USB or take the SDChip and plug into slot.

Open with Picasa Select all Photos and download Photos.

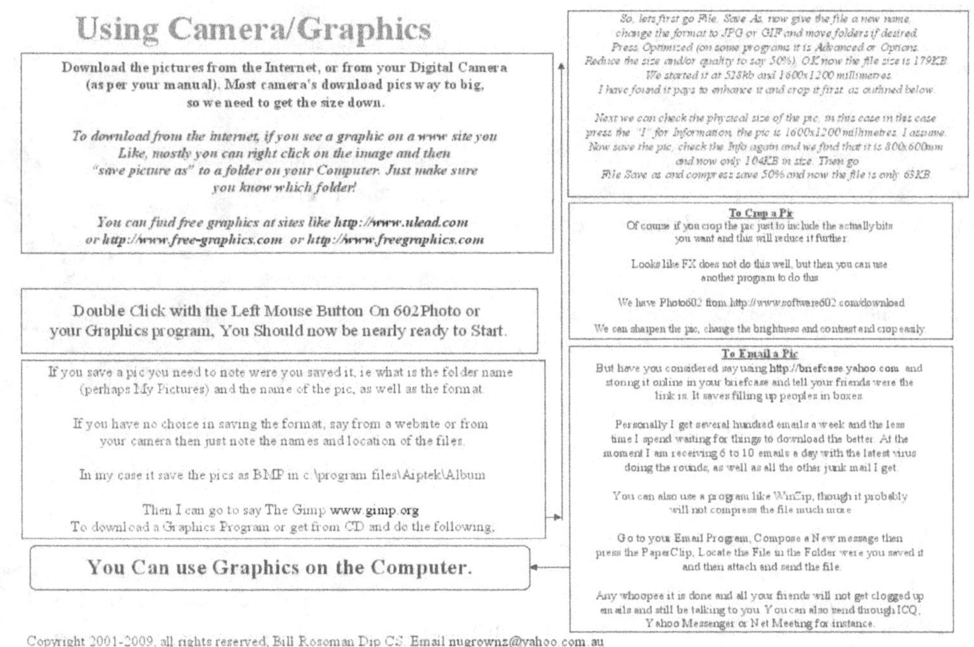

Make sure you safely remove USB Devices by Clicking on the USB Icon on the Toolbar and Click on Safely Remove Hardware. If you do not you may loose any information you have copied. Especially if the Devices is busy.

Skype Internet Telephone, Video Calls

To maker phone calls, conference calls and video calls online or to call people on Skype.

www.skype.com

Log onto the Internet, Open Skype and Log on.

Select a contact from the list, or add a contact or dial a number.

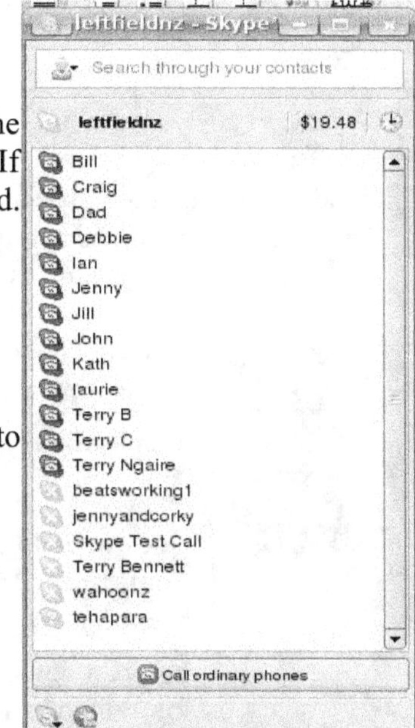

Numbering is in the format +6468999999 64 is the Country code for NZ 1 is for the USA, the next 6 is the area code then the Telephone number,

The cost for a call Computer to Computer is free, for a call Computer to a Landline is round 3 cents a minute. for a call Computer to a Mobile is around 20+ cents a minute.

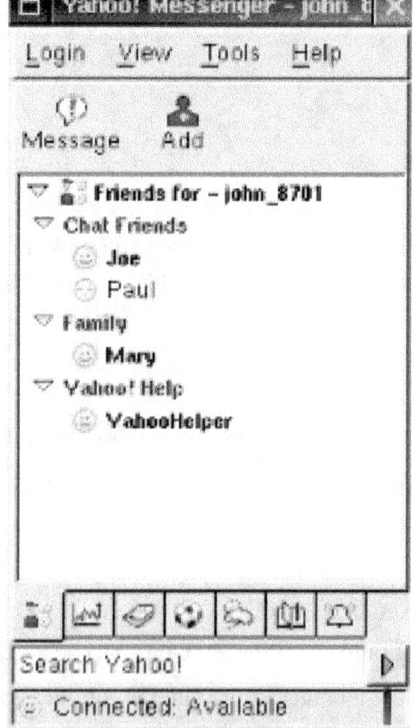

You can call people who only have a landline or mobile. Although this costs (You need to Buy a 10 Euro card from Skype and it cost around 3 cents per minute to NZ and more for mobiles).

You have to have a Skype ID and Password (you can sign up on their website and it is all free). My ID is leftfieldnz. Then you login and can chat to friends and do dozens of other things like share conversations, webcams, photos, files etc etc.

Open Skype and Logon if asked.

Goto Tool Create a Conference Call. Add the Friends you wish to Conference with and press Start.

I am pretty sure you can include people who only have a landline or mobile. Although this costs (You need to Buy a 10 Euro card from Skype and it cost around 3 cents per minute)

You and your Friends/Associates only need to have a Computer with access to the Internet (Dial up is OK, but Broadband is better), or access to a computer or if the worst is to be a Phone or Cell Phone. And then you can Chat, Share Webcams, Photos, Files Etc.

Yahoo Messenger

One way to Communicate and have Conference Calls Online, is to use Yahoo Messenger.

You can download the required software for Windows/Linux/Mac and use it that way (Picture on Left). Or you use it from a webpage @ www.meebo.com (Picture on Right). Or from a 3G Mobile

You have to have a Yahoo ID and Password (you can sign up on their website and it is all free). My ID is leftfieldnz. Then you login and can chat to friends and do dozens of other things like share conversations, webcams, photos, files etc etc.

Or you can have a Conference Call You can even use Yahoo Messenger on a mobile Even when you're out, you're in. Yahoo! Messenger keeps you connected even when you're away from your PC. There are two ways to use Yahoo! Messenger with your mobile phone: Send IMs as text messages from your PC to your friends' mobile phones Sign into Yahoo! Messenger from your mobile phone and send IMs to your friends when you're away from your PC

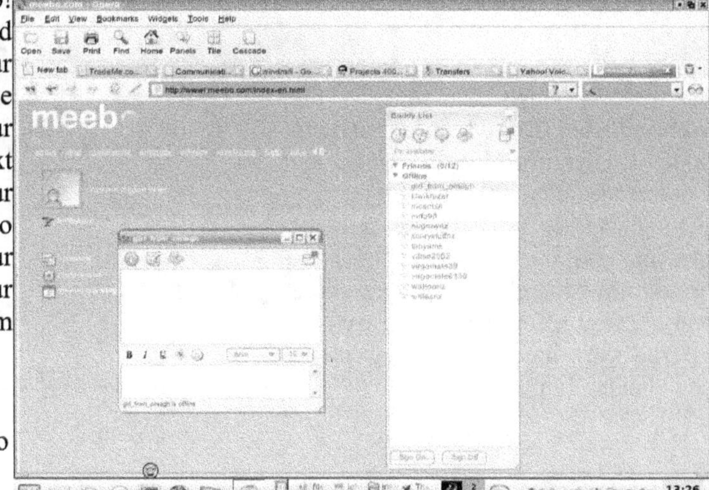

To start using Yahoo! Messenger right from your phone, find out

1. Click the Conference button in the IM window.

2. Invite friends by clicking their names from your Messenger List and selecting Add.

3. Invite someone not on your Messenger List by clicking Invite Other.

4. Once your friends accept your invitation, you can all message in the same window.

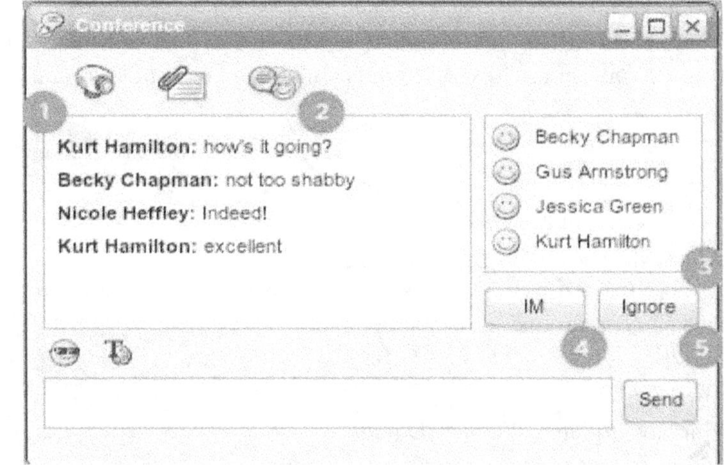

which version works best for your phone model, it's easy! Go to Yahoo! Mobile Choose your carrier Enter your phone brand and model

Get Yahoo! Messenger on your mobile phone and get going!

Conference Call It's easy to have a conversation with multiple people when you use Conference in Yahoo! Messenger. Communicate via text in one window, or share your webcam with several people at once.

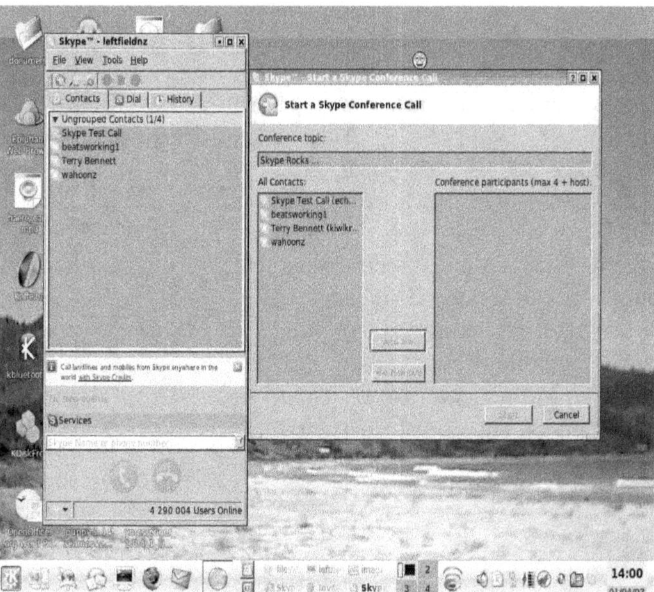

(1) Enable video by clicking the Webcam icon. (2) Add more friends to your Conference by clicking the Conference icon. (3) The conference participants are listed to the right of the conversation. (4) Send a friend a private IM by highlighting their name and clicking IM. (5) Ignore a friend's messages by highlighting their name and clicking Ignore.

Skype VOIP.

You can download the required software for Windows/Linux/Mac and use it that way (Picture on Right). You can use Skype for calls Online and to Landlines and Cellphones. Computer to Computer is free.

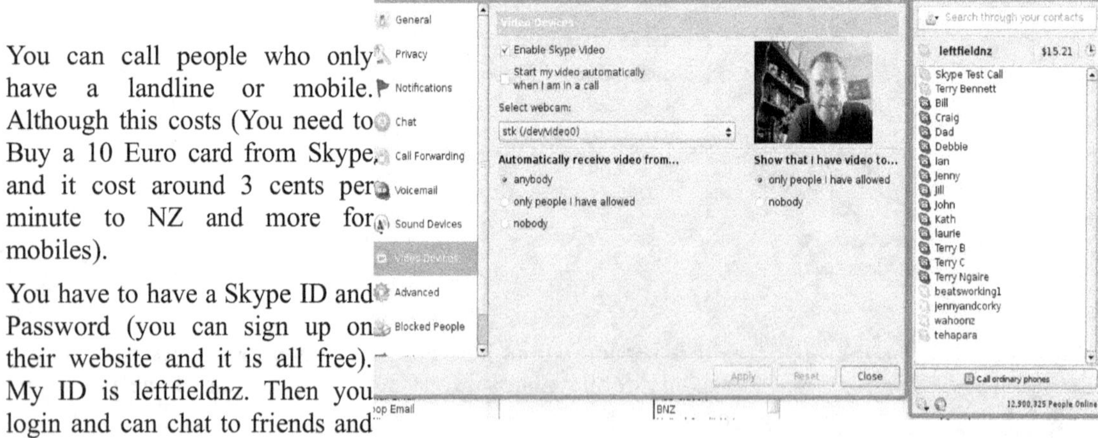

You can call people who only have a landline or mobile. Although this costs (You need to Buy a 10 Euro card from Skype, and it cost around 3 cents per minute to NZ and more for mobiles).

You have to have a Skype ID and Password (you can sign up on their website and it is all free). My ID is leftfieldnz. Then you login and can chat to friends and do dozens of other things like share conversations, webcams, photos, files etc etc.

Skype Conference Call

Open Skype and Logon if asked. Goto Tool Create a Conference Call. Add the Friends you wish to Conference with and press Start.

I am pretty sure you can include people who only have a landline or mobile. Although this costs (You need to Buy a 10 Euro card from Skype and it cost around 3 cents per minute)

You can also use a webcam with Programs like Skype and Yahoo Messenger.

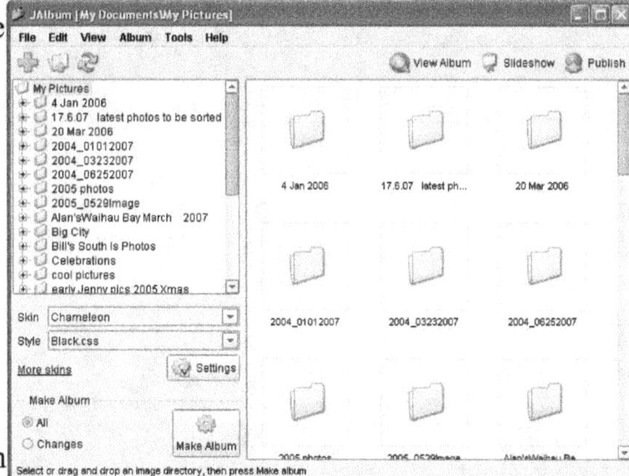

Skype also does Video with your Webcam.

Jalbum

Makes all you pictures into a nice Album which can be viewed like a webpage or burnt to CD/DVD for viewing on a DVD player.

Open Jalbum

Select a Skin

Click the Green Plus to add Folders and/or Files

Click on Make Album

Wait a wee while and that's it.

To Download stuff from the Internet

There are many ways to download from the Internet, a simple Google search for Free DVD Player Software, is one way. Sites like http://www.freewarehome.com or www.download.com are also good places to start.

Locate the files you wish to Download and Click on it and Save to your Computer.

Cut and Paste Stuff

Basic Cutting and Pasting in and to and from MS Word, MS Excel, MS Explorer, MS Internet Explorer, Firefox, Open Office, or Your Favourite Program, and most Windows programs is the same.

The same in Linux, most of these Commands are universal.

<u>Basic Key Board Commands</u>

CTRL+A   Select All Text and or Objects

CTRL+C   Copy to Clipboard
CTRL+X   Move to Clipboard
CTRL+V   Paste from Clipboard

To Cut and Paste

Select the object and/or text to be copied/moved, for the whole lot use CTRL+A
or the use the mouse or Press Shift and use Cursor Keys to highlight.

Press CTRL+C or +X to Copy or Move.
Goto new location or new program and Press CTRL+V to Paste and it is all over.

OR you can use the Mouse;

Left click and sweep the text or object. Right Click and Copy to Clipboard
Go to new program location, Right Click and Paste. Or Right Click and Delete the File.

You can have several programs open, like a Graphics Program And a Word Processing Program to Cut & Paste Between them.

Use ALT+TAB to move between Programs.
Or Use Explore by Right Clicking on Start and opening "Explore"

Usually you use Windows Explore to look around the computer and to access CD and A: Floppy Disks etc.

Right click on Start and select Explore (If toolbar not available press CTRL+ESC, select Programmes and Windows Explore).

On the left you will see the Tree of Drives and Folders in those drives. On the right you will see folders and files that are in the Folder or Drive that is highlighted on the left pane.

Phew easy aye!

Now say you want to copy a file from you CD to your Hard Drive C:

OK open Windows Explore as outlined above

Move down the left hand pane of Explore and locate the CD, it looks like a little CD and is probably called D: E: or maybe F: or M: but any way is usually the last drive on the left hand pane.

Click on the CD and you should hear the CD start up and the CD light come on

You should soon see folders and files that are on the CD

Now you can copy files and move them to you Hard Drive or install a programme from the CD

Lets try one

Say you want to install a programme that is on the CD

Locate the file on the CD and then double click on it with the Left Mouse Button or click on it and press enter. Normal the file will be called something.exe or install.exe or setup.exe.

You should see the file open and start to install the programme. You will be prompted for some information and you should just follow the on screen instructions and the programme should install OK.

If things do not go according to plan then you may need to clean the CD player or CD or it may pay to copy the file to your hard drive then install it.

Lets try that, copy a file or files from the CD to your computer.

Locate the file on the CD and then single click on it with the Left Mouse Button or hold down shift and select several files with the mouse or cursor. If the files are not together (non-contiguous) then hold down the CTRL button and select the files by pressing the SHIFT key.

OK Now press CTRL+C to copy the files to the clipboard. You can also use the right mouse button and select copy or Edit Copy from the Menu.

So we now have these files on the clipboard and can now locate the place we wish them to go.

On the left Pane of Explore locate the location you wish to copy the files to say C:\My Downloads (C: would denote the hard drive of your computer, you may have D: or E: as well).

If the folder is not there then you may have to create one. Click on C: in the left pane to and select File, New, Folder, and a new folder should appear in the Right Pane at the bottom, rename it My Downloads by typing in the words. If you cannot then highlight the folder press F2 and type in the words.

Now the folder is then highlighted in the left pane of explore, now press CTRL+V to paste or right click and select paste or use Edit paste from the menu.

You should see the files appear at the bottom of the right pane of explore.

Great you have copied them.

Now you can use them if they are data files like a Word Document or install them if they are an EXE file. (This denotes and Executable file).

Fun Fun in the Sun!

The same can be done from A: or B: usually the Floppy Drives.

OK now some other tricks. If the file you are copying ends in .ZIP then it is compressed file and needs to be unzipped before you can use the files or programme it contains.

Now when you open the file you can then extract it to say C:\temp by select it in the left or locate it on the hard drive.

Once the file is extracted then go to the place were you unzipped it and the files or program will be available for you.

OK cool as cats for now!!!

These are the instructions to cut and paste files using Explore or other Windows based programmes.

Other Very Common Commands.

CTRL+P	Print
CTRL+S	Save
CTRL+O	Open
ALT+F4	Exit
CTRL+N	New Doc
CTRL+F	Find
CTRL+H	Replace
F5	Go to
F9	Recalc

F1   Help

Cut and Paste Objects/Files

Basic Cutting and Pasting in and to and from MS Word, MS Excel, MS Explorer,
MS Internet Explorer, Firefox, or Your Favourite Program,
and most Windows programmes is the same.

Basic Key Board Commands

CTRL+A   Select All Text and or Objects   CTRL+C Copy to Clipboard
CTRL+X   Move to Clipboard   CTRL+V   Paste from Clipboard

To Cut and Paste

Select the object and/or text to be copied/moved, for the whole lot use CTRL+A
or the use the mouse or Press Shift and use Cursor Keys to highlight.

Press CTRL+C or +X to Copy or Move.
Goto new location or new programme and Press CTRL+V to Paste and it is all over.

OR you can use the Mouse:

Left click and sweep the text or object, Right Click and Copy to Clipboard
Go to new programme location, Right Click and Paste. Or Right Click and Delete the File.

You can have several programs open, like a Graphics Program
And a Word Processing Program to Cut & Paste Between them.
Use ALT+TAB to move between Programs.
Or Use Explore by Right Clicking on Start and opening "Explore"

For more information Go to
www.webng.com/leftfieldnz
(Do not put www. In front).

Your File should now be Deleted or Moved.

Open Office Quick Start

You can Open the Open Office Quick Start Menu from the Icon on the Desktop or on the Toolbar (bottom right of Desktop). Select the Type of File you want and click on the Icon.

Comparison Between Microsoft Office and Open Office

Function	*MS Office*	*Open Office*
Database	MS Access	Open Office Base
Spreadsheet	MS Excel	Open Office Calc
Word-processing	MS Word	Open Office Writer
Presentation	MS Powerpoint	Open Office Impress
Drawing		Open Office Draw
Advanced Maths		Open Office Math

The two main Office Suites are Microsoft Office (MS Office) and Open Office (O Office or Open Office) The main differences are;

- MS Office is proprietary (nothing much can be changed), Open Office is Open Source and can be altered by anybody with some programming knowledge
- MS Office you have to pay for, Open Office is Free.
- the two products are similar in use and commands are similar.
- Ms Office does some things well as does Open Office
- MS Office only runs in Windows and Mac, Open Office runs in multi-platforms Windows, Linux Mac etc.
- MS Office is maintained by Microsoft, no one else can do much, Open Office is maintained by a Project Team and the Community and anyone can make or suggest changes.

The two Office Suites are OK and both have strengths and weaknesses.

The advantage of OO is that it is Free and is Supported by the Whole Community.

OO is the Office Suite of Choice for Linux.

The Beginning, How to get Started

Most Beginners/Learners seem to get in deep trouble quick using the Office Suite, either MS Office or Open Office.

If you have MS Office or Open Office Installed then we are diving right into the deep end! If you do not have MS Office or Open Office then look on the Internet and you will see the Windows and Linux versions of Open Office (the Free one).

When finished, to access Open Office got to > Start > Programs > open Office.org > Select the Program you want.

The big secret for me in using MS Office or Open Office is start at the end and work backwards from there. It is a bit counter-intuitive but it certainly makes life easier.

So the first question to ask is what are you trying to Achieve and How do you want the final Product to look. This will determine which Program of the Office Suite you will use and then how you layout the Document when you decide which Program to use.

Most Beginners seem to pick Word/Writer and try and do everything in that. Which is fine to a point. But if you have a lot of pictures or many tables of numbers perhaps it will get very unwieldy very quickly and may become a huge mess and very hard to achieve what you set out to do.

Lets consider some scenarios;

You want a document that mainly contains words and numbers, but not too many pictures or tables etc.

      You would Choose Word/Writer.

You want a document that contains words and numbers, and many pictures or tables etc.

      You would Choose Impress/Powerpoint or perhaps Word/Writer.

You want a document that contains numbers, and graphs, storing say addresses etc.

      You would Choose Calc/Excel.

You want a document that will be a Presentation, and has many pictures, videos etc.

      You would Choose Impress/Powerpoint.

You want a document that contains lots of Data, and you want to manipulate the Data etc.

You would Choose Base/Access.

A lot of people just try and do everything in Writer/Word, but that can be too hard compared with what some of the other Programs can do.

You can also marry information from the different programs into other programs.

IE Doing numbers in Calc/Excel and importing a graph into Impress/Powerpoint.

How to write a Document/Letter

Welcome and lets hope these instructions make it fun and easy to use the Computer to do some Typing.

First lets make sure the Computer is plugged into the power outlet and the power is switched on at the Wall.
Now Turn on the Computer and Screen.

Hopefully you get to the Desktop OK and ready to Rock and Roll!

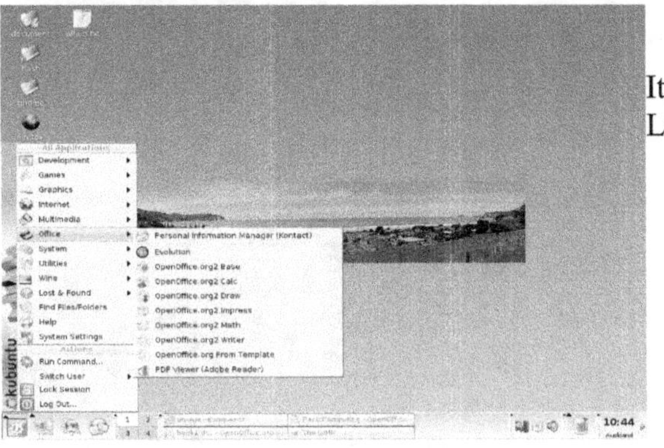

It should look something like this Picture (My Linux Desktop).

Now from the Start Menu (Bottom Left of Desktop), Select the Program you wish to use.

In Linux (Kubuntu running KDE), Use > Start > Office > Writer etc.

In Windows Start > All Programs > Open Office > OO Wordprocessor

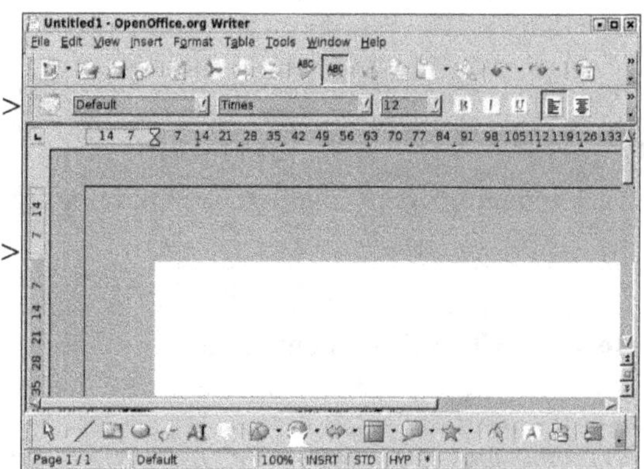

You should now see, a Blank Document or Select Ctrl+N for a *New Document.*

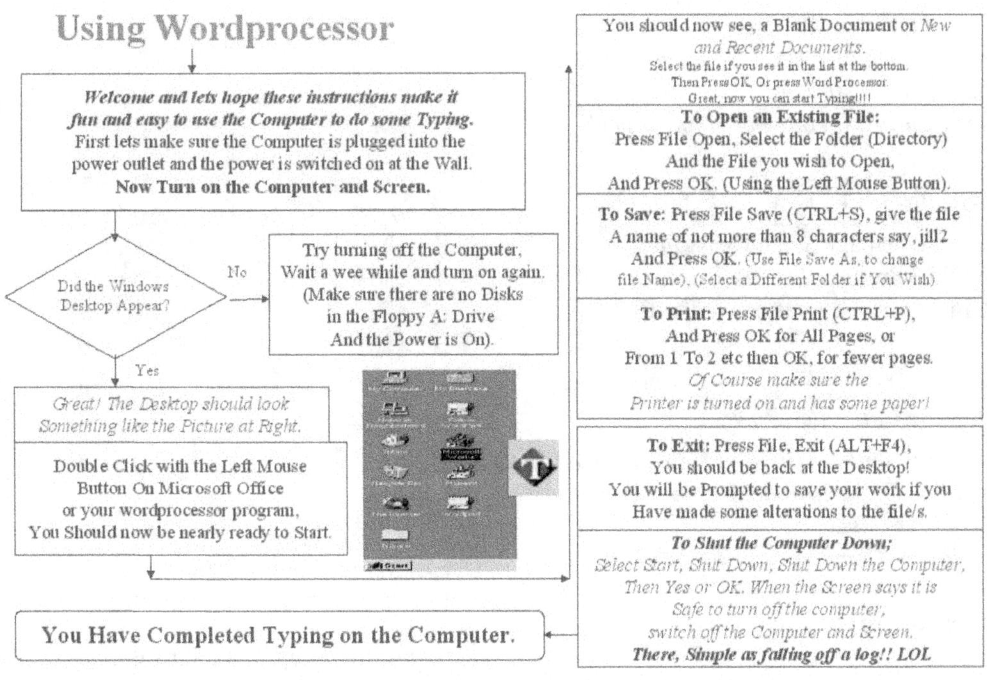

From the File Menu > Select a Recently Opened File if you see it in the list at the bottom.
Then Press OK, Or press Word Processor.

Great, now you can start Typing!!!!

To Open an Existing File:

Press File Open (Ctrl+O), Select the Folder (Directory)
And the File you wish to Open,
And Press OK. (Using the Left Mouse Button).

To Save: Press File Save (CTRL+S), give the file

A name of not more than 8 characters say, jill2
And Press OK. (Use File Save As, to change
file Name), (Select a Different Folder if You Wish).

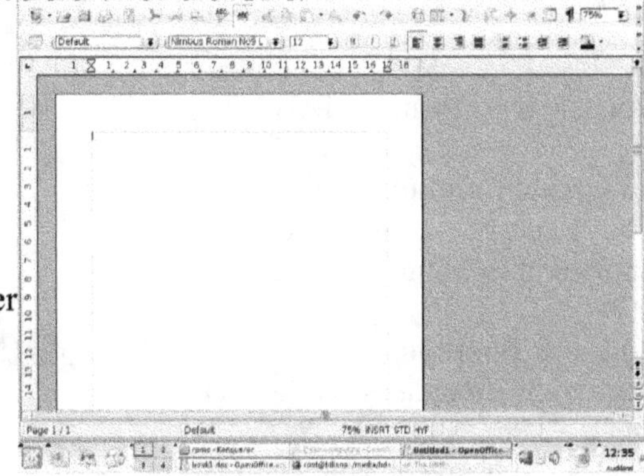

To Print: Press File Print (CTRL+P),

And Press OK for All Pages, or
From 1 To 2 etc then OK, for fewer pages.
Of Course make sure the
Printer is turned on and has some paper!

To Exit: Press File, Exit (ALT+F4),

You should be back at the Desktop!
You will be Prompted to save your work if you
Have made some alterations to the file/s.

To Shut the Computer Down;

Select Start, Shut Down, Shut Down the Computer,
Then Yes or OK. When the Screen says it is
Safe to turn off the computer,
switch off the Computer and Screen.

To Insert a Graphic/Picture
Select > Insert >Picture from File. Locate the Folder were the Graphic/Picture is (use Preview to have a sneak view) > Select the Pic and Press Open/OK

To Insert a Table

use Insert > Table > Select how many columns and then OK.
You add rows by using TAB.

To Create Columns
Use > Format > Page > Columns > Set
number of Columns and OK

To Use a Template
Locate the Templates on the CD, Open
and the Use > File Save As and Select a
Folder and Name on your Hard Drive.

Use the Template as suggested.

There, Simple as falling off a log!! LOL

Open Office Does;

1. Word-processing
2. Spreadsheets
3. Presentations
4. Drawing
5. Web Pages
6. Formula
7. Labels
8. Business Cards
9. Templates
10. Envelopes
11. Data Bases

To be able to read on a Windows Machine, save the file as MS Word or Excel. Or perhaps as a PDF File.

These are the Basic Command Short Cuts, of Cause you can go File > Save with you mouse but the Keyboard Short Cuts are so much easier and better on the hands.

How to Create a Spreadsheet

Hopefully you have got to the Desktop OK and ready to Rock and Roll!

If not check the "How to Write a Document/letter" Section for more Information.

Now from the Start Menu (Bottom Left of Desktop), Select the Program you wish to use.

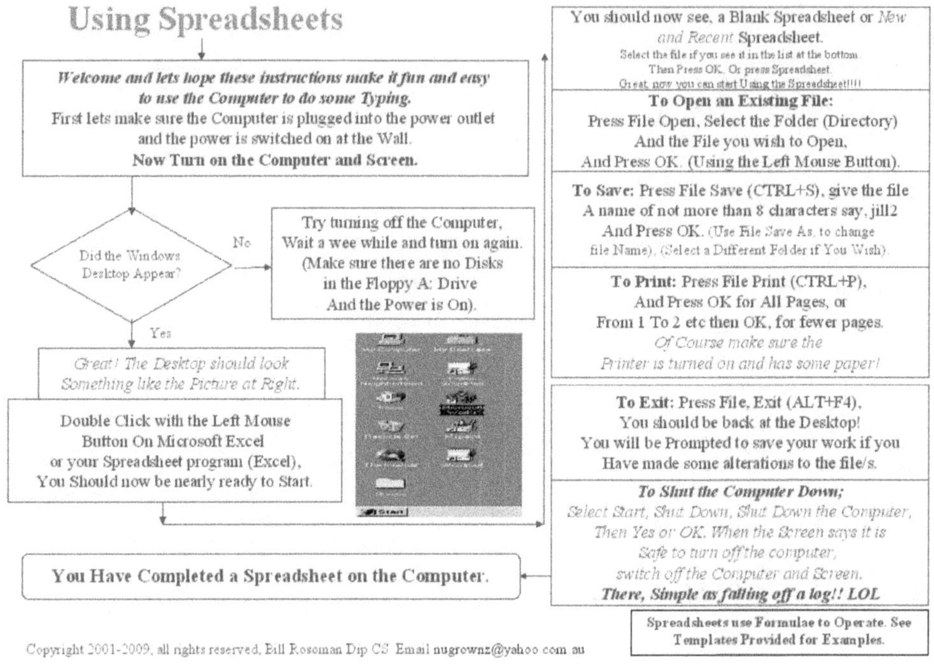

In Linux (Kubuntu running KDE), Use > Start > Office > Open Office Spreadsheet
In Windows Start > All Programs > Open Office > OO Calc

You should now see, a Blank Document or Select Ctrl+N for a New Document.

From the File Menu > Select a Recently Opened File if you see it in the list at the bottom.
Then Press OK, Or press Word Processor.

Great, now you can start Creating Your Spreadsheet!!!!

This is a simple Budget Spreadsheet.
It is fairly simple to set up and use.

Set up some headings

Bill Rosoman
Gisborne NZ

Budget
2005

Item	Expense	Item	Income

Enter some Items and Amounts

Item		Expense
Wages		20.00
General Improvements		45.00
Resources		55.00
Running costs		66.00
	Petrol	77.00
	Phone	20.00
	Rent	45.00
Staff Development		3,000.00
Travel - Networking		3,000.00
Technology		3,000.00

Down the bottom is some Formula

Total Income =	###
Total Expenses =	###
Income - Expenses =	8,169.00

BTW The ### above shows that the cell is to narrow and hiding the figures. Make the cell a bit wider.

Nugrow Technologies
Gisborne NZ
2001

Item		Expense	Item	Income
Wages		20.00	Cash	4,000.00
General Improvements		45.00	Investments	500.00
Resources		55.00	Misc	1,000.00
Running costs		66.00		
	Petrol	77.00		
	Phone	20.00		
	Rent	45.00		
Staff Development		3,000.00		
Travel - Networking		3,000.00		
Technology		3,000.00		
Professional Affiliations		2,000.00		
Advertising		2,000.00		
R&D		2.00		
R&M Vehicles		1.00		
R&M Buildings				
Misc.				
Food				
Depreciation				
Stationery				
Photocopying				
Fees				
Insurance				
IRD				
Tax				
Postage				
Freight				

The Formula look like this

=SUM(G22:G42)

=SUM(C22:C63)

=F50-F51

Total Income =	**5,500.00**
Total Expenses =	**13,331.00**
Income - Expenses =	**-7,831.00**

Then Save the file

Set the Print Area,

Format > Print Range > Add

Save again and you are away!

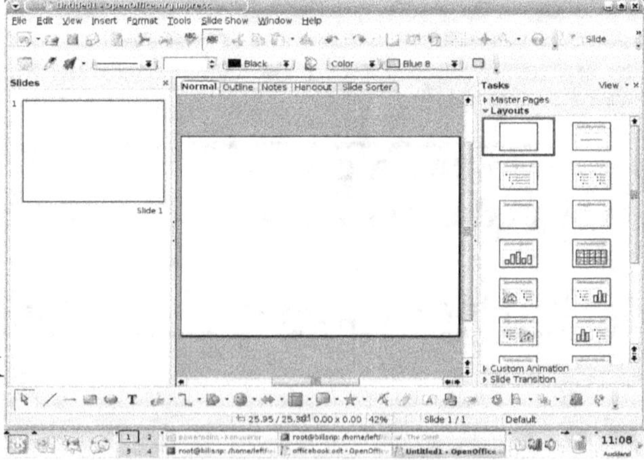

How to Create a Presentation

Hopefully you have got to the Desktop OK and ready to Rock and Roll!

If not check the "How to Write a Document/letter" Section for more Information.

Now from the Start Menu (Bottom Left of Desktop), Select the Program you wish to use.

In Linux (Kubuntu running KDE), Use > Start > Office > Impress etc.

In Windows Start > All Programs > Open Office > OO Impress

Or use the Quickstart Option on the Toolbar at the Bottom Right of the Desktop.

Now you can Create a New Presentation > Use a Template > Or open an Existing Presentation.

From the File Menu > Select a Recently Opened File if you see it in the list at the bottom.
Then Press OK..

Great, now you can start Creating Your Presentation!!!!

You could just start with a blank Presentation and then Click on the Layout that suits the Slide you want to Create, then fill in with Text, Video, Audio, Graphics Etc.

Or you could use a Template

If want every Slide to look the Same, Use the Master Slide and Put the Layout, the Background, what Fonts, Header or Footer, etc and this will appear on every slide.

Press F5 to View the Presentation.

How to Create a Database

Hopefully you have got to the Desktop OK and ready to Rock and Roll!

If not check the "How to Write a Document/letter" Section for more Information.

It should look something like this Picture (My Linux Desktop).

Now from the Start Menu (Bottom Left of Desktop), Select the Program you wish to use.

In Linux (Kubuntu running KDE), Use > Start > Office > Base etc.
In Windows Start > All Programs > Open Office > OO Base

Or use the Quickstart Option on the Toolbar at the Bottom Right of the Desktop.

From the Opening screen you can Create a New Database, Open an Existing Database.

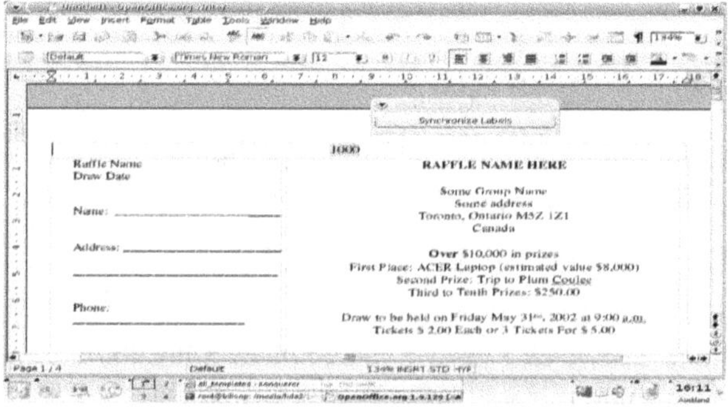

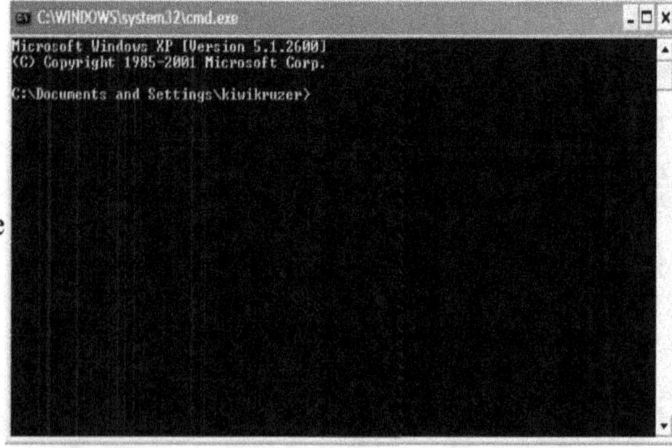

To Make a DVD Movie

We are using DVDStyler, ffmpeg, Photostage Slideshow Producer, vlc and infrarecorder.

(they are all free and legal software)

http://www.dvdstyler.de/

http://ffdshow.faireal.net/mirror/ffmpeg
http://www.nchsoftware.com/slideshow/index.html
http://infrarecorder.sourceforge.net/
http://www.videolan.org/

Download Movies from Your Camera as usual

Convert to DVD-PAL

start

run

cmd

OK

Type in cd \bill\ffmpeg

Type in

ffmpeg -i \bill\movies\100_2747.MOV -y
-target   pal-dvd   -b   1800
\bill\movies\mov1.mpg

Or the location of your movies

Use TAB to complete operation

like \bi then TAB will complete the rest

Use the up arrow and change the video names
and go again

cd ..

Takes you up one folder

Create a DVD

Use dvdstyler

Create Title and sub-titles

Click on Right Window

Add Text

Create a headline "Terry's Video"

Click OK

Right Click on Title

Select Properties

Change Font Parameters

Add a Background

Always add the Background Last!

Can be any picture/photo

Right click on Background and Arrange > Send to Back

Burn DVD

Create DVD in DVD Styler

Either Burn straight to DVD or Create DVD Folder

Use DVD Burner infrarecorder and Burn DVD-Video

Copy the Folder VIDEO_VTS to the DVD-Video and burn.

Create a Slideshow

Use Photostage Slideshow Producer

Add Photos by Insert Slides

Add Sound Track/Music by Set Sound Track

Build Slideshow > Windows PC > Browse, were do you want to save to (give location and file name) > Format .mpg > Build Slideshow

Video Player

VLC is an excellent Video Player.

Google Earth

You need to have the proper 3D graphics card installed and the appropriate drivers to run Google Earth.

Download and Install from Google.

www.google.com

The new Google Earth is amazing. You now have Google Earth, Sky and Photos as well as a new Ocean Overlay. Truly Amazing!

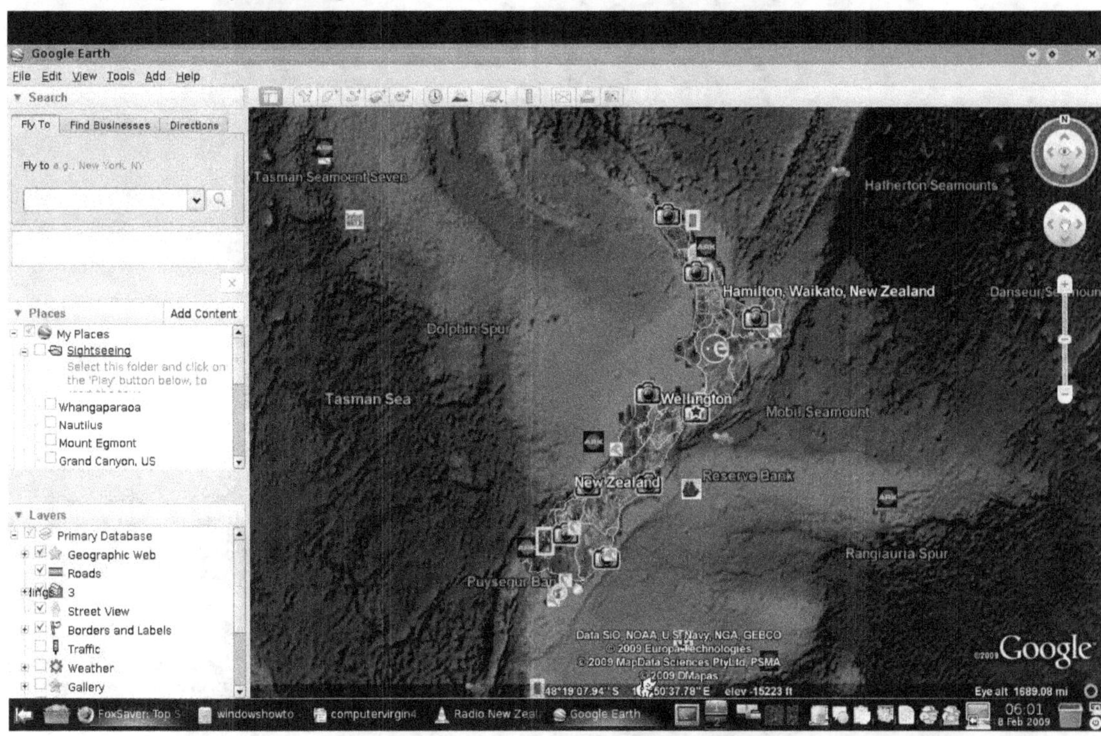

This Wayne's Boat at Tokomaru Bay. 100Km North of Gisborne, New Zealand.

3D of Mount Egmont/Taranaki from Google Earth.

If you Click on the Icon at the top you also have Google Sky.

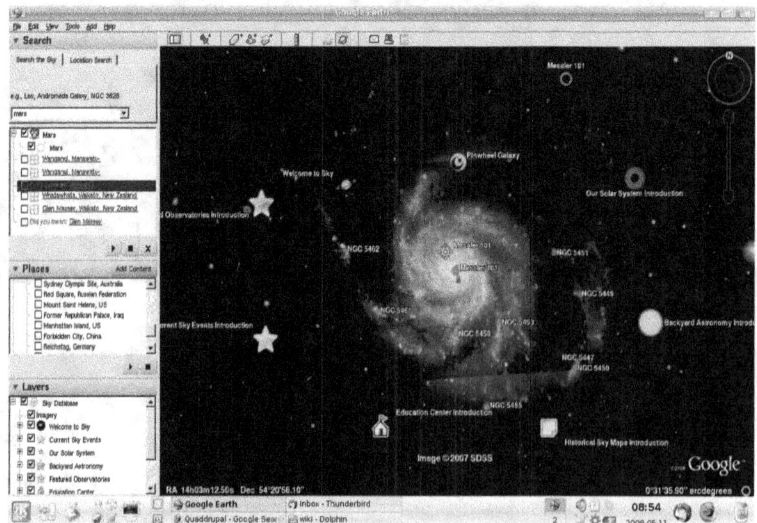

Funny also you can fly the globe, Under Tools > Flight Simulator.

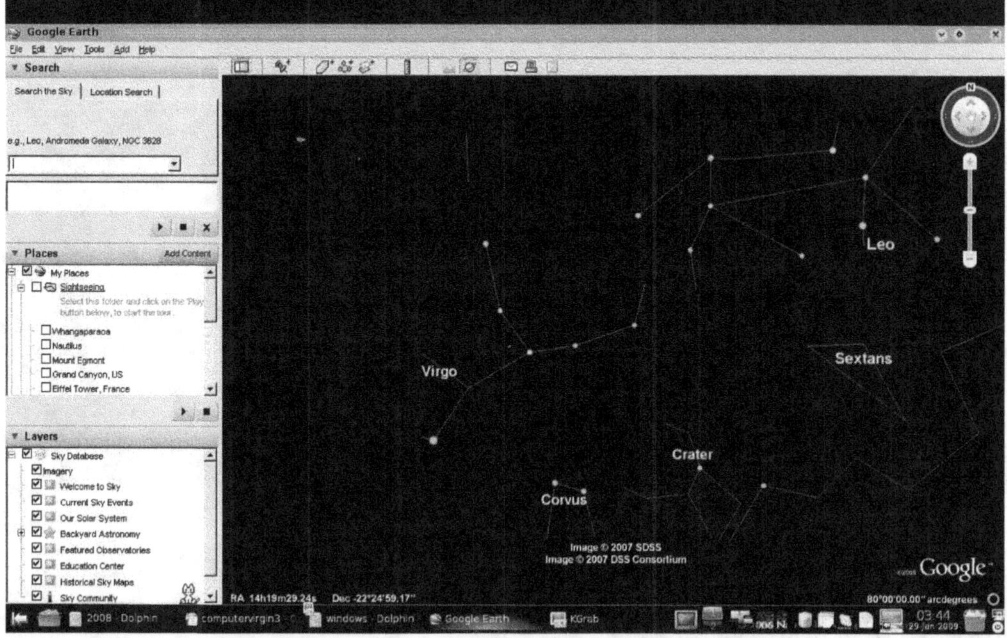

The latest Google Thing is Google View. You got to Google Maps. http://maps.google.com and go to an address and then Press the Google View Icon and you will with a bit of luck see the buildings at that location.

This is the house were I grew up and if you do a 180 you will see the park I played as a kid.

Planning Your Trip/Finding Directions Using Google

Have you tried Google to get directions for your next trip

There are two ways to use google to get directions for your trip.

Google Maps @ http://maps.google.com/ Is the easiest and can be done on any computer with access to the internet. BTW this is all for free.

Open your favourite Web Browser, log onto the Internet (if you have to) Type in the Web Address above and you should be @ Google Maps. Click on the Directions Button and enter

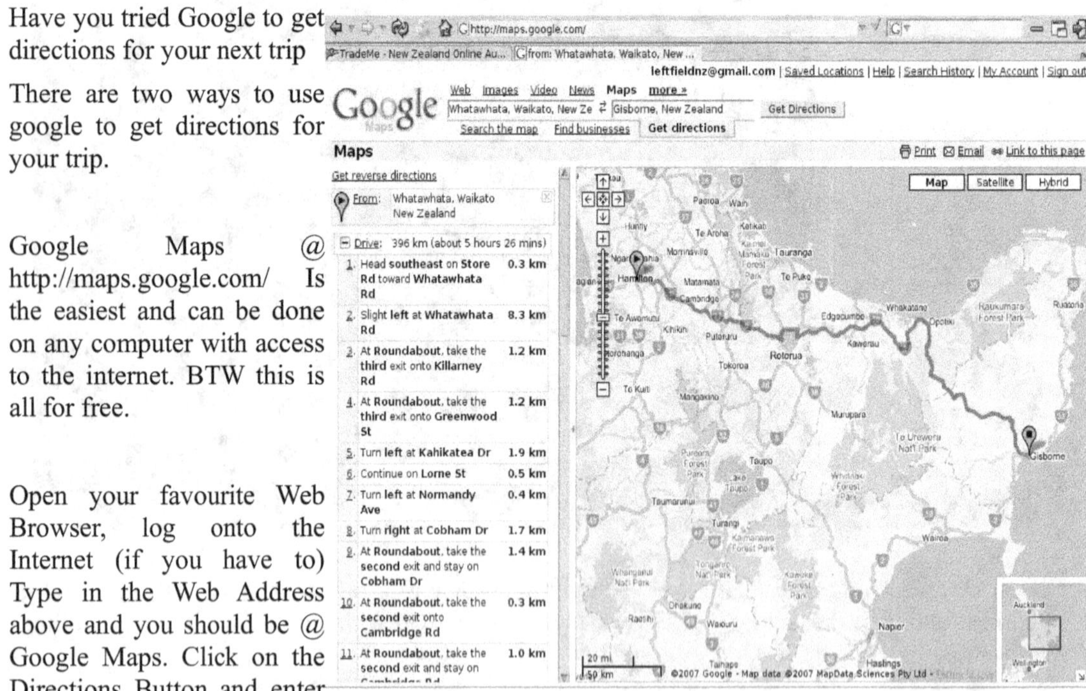

the From and To Locations, always followed by New Zealand, IE Hamilton New Zealand, as there are about 20 odd Hamitons' in the world!

To capture the directions, you can Print them, Go File Save as so they are on your computer or Press Print Screen and Open in your favourite graphics program and Save As a Graphic. You could then save the graphic to your MP4 Player and have on hand on your travels.

The other option is Google Earth @ http://earth.google.com/

Were you download some software and then run that software to get directions

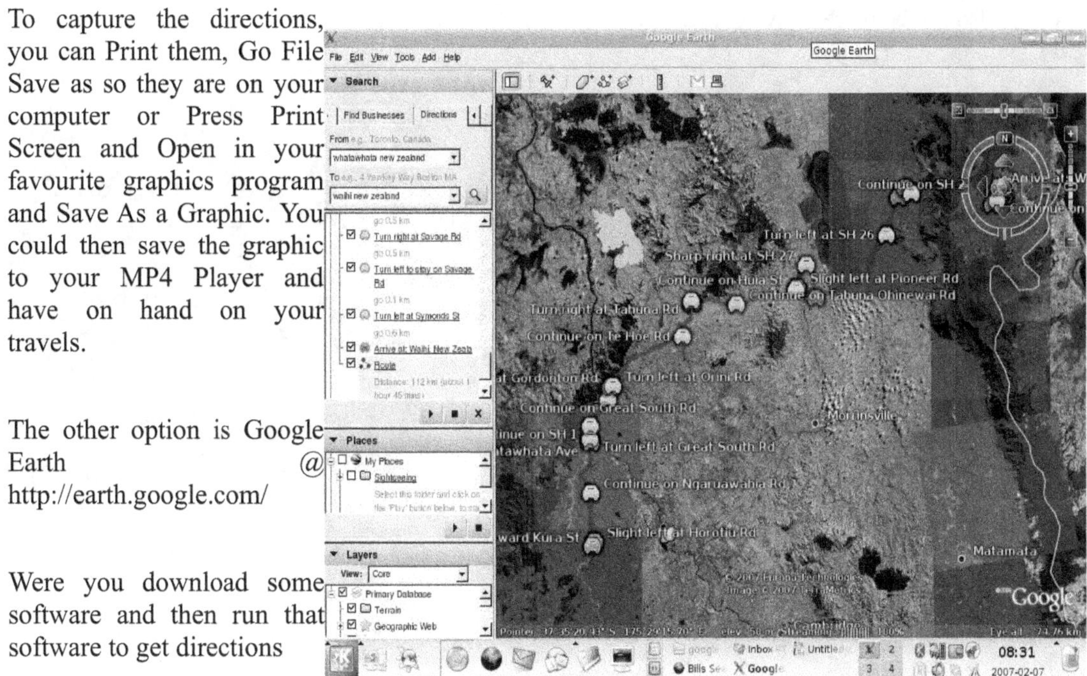

Open Google Earth, Click on the Directions Button (top left)., Type in the From and To locations using wherever New Zealand format. Press Search and now you have a detailed map giving you directions.

Again this can be printed, stored on computer or transferred to your MP4 Player.

Google Earth will work on dial up, if you have plenty of patience, but is better on fast internet (broadband)

Using a Mobile Telephone Online

If your are away from home and want to keep in touch the way to it is use your Cell Phone Online

Most large providers like Google and Yahoo have special pages for Mobile WAP users.

I have a WAP page on my website as well as the same sites Bookmarked on my Cell Phone.

You will also notice there are websites just for Mobile WAP Phones.

This is my WAP Page Online.

www.webng.com/leftfieldnz/wap.html

Bills WAP Page

http://www.google.com/wml	Google
http://www.grabbit.co.nz	Grabbit
http://www.infogo.com	Infogo
http://wap.yahoo.co.uk	Yahoo
http://www.wapcardz.com	wapcardz
http://www.yourwap.com	yourwap
http://mobile.gmail.com	gmail
http://www.wapsilion.com	wapsilion
http://wap.oa.yahoo.com/	Yahoo Mail
http://news.bbc.co.uk/1/low	BBC
http://www.vodafone.co.nz	vodafone
www.twitter.com/home	Twitter
www.webng.com/leftfieldnz	leftfieldnz
www.voanews.com/english/mobile	Voice of America
www.picasaweb.google.com/m/	Picasa Pictures
www.m.youtube.com/	You Tube
www.m.trademe.con.nz	Trade Me
www.radionz.co.nz/news/home	Radio New Zealand

Cell Phone Secrets
*#06# Cell Phone Serial Number
To activate Call Holding:
 Firstly, Call Holding must be activated on your SIM Card.
 You can activate your SIM Card from you cellphone by doing the following:·

* Activate: *43# (green phone/yes/OK).

* Cancel: #43# (green phone/yes/OK).

Once active, Call Waiting lets you know there's another call waiting by making a "beep" sound. You simply put your first call on hold by pressing 2 (green phone/yes/OK). Then take the second call. To return to your first call or to witch between calls - press 2 (green phone/yes/'OK). You also have the option to end the first call before taking the new call. To do this press 1 (green phone/yes/OK). Or, you can ignore the waiting call without disturbing the present call by pressing 0 (green phone/yes/OK).

Change your PIN code by doing this:·

* Press **04*#.·

* Enter the old PIN code (00000 at first) then press *·

* Next, enter your new secret PIN code, followed by the * button. Choose a number that you will remember easily. It can be up to 8 numbers long but not less than 4. Most people choose 4 numbers.

* Enter the new number again and press #.

* Every time you switch your cell phone on it will ask you to enter this secret PIN code.

• You can change your number whenever you want, by using the above instructions.

How to unblock your cellphone:

Your SIM Card will become "blocked" if the wrong PIN code is entered into your cellphone 3 times. Make your SIM Card in your cellphone work again by using the PUK number (printed on the same sticker that contains your cellphone number) and follow these easy instructions:

* Press **05*.

* Then enter your PUK number and then the * button.

* Enter a new PIN, then press *.

* Enter the new PIN again and press #.

ISSUE: Can I call for Emergency services?

Solution:

Emergency Services

Emergency Services 111 (in New Zealand). A 24-hour crisis centre for any emergency. Whether you need to police an ambulance or other emergency help.

How to use this service

* Call Emergency Services 111 - Dial 111 from your Cell phone. Give your name to the operator. Give as much detail as you can of your emergency situation and needs. Assistance will be dispatched to you. A follow-up call will be made to ensure that you have been assisted.

The emergency Services 111 number works even when you have no SIM card and/ or he is not sure of the PIN number.

So you can take a picture on your cell phone and either email to someone, or send it by Bluetooth to our Computer, or upload it straight to a website like Picasa Pictures.

This is the Source code for my WAP page.

There is other ways of doing a WAP page but this way works for my Cell Phone.

```
<!DOCTYPE html PUBLIC "-//W3C//DTD XHTML 1.0 Transitional//EN"
"http://www.w3.org/TR/xhtml1/DTD/xhtml1-transitional.dtd">
<html>
<head>
 <meta http-equiv="Content-Type" content="text/html; charset=UTF-8" />
 <meta name="robots" content="index,follow" />
 <meta name="keywords" content="Bill, WAP" />
<meta name="description" content="Bill's WAP Page." />
</head>
<body>
Bills WAP Page

<ul>
 <li class="rc-major">
   <a href="http://www.google.com/wml" google="" class="wiki">Google</a>
 </li>
 <li class="rc-major"><a href="http://www.grabbit.co.nz" grabbit="" class="wiki">Grabbit</a>
 </li>
 <li class="rc-major"><a href="http://www.infogo.com" infogo="" class="wiki">Infogo</a>
 </li>
 <li class="rc-major"><a href="http://wap.yahoo.co.uk" yahoo="" class="wiki">Yahoo</a>
 </li>
 <li class="rc-major"><a href="http://www.wapcardz.com" wapcardz=""
class="wiki">wapcardz</a>
 </li>
 <li class="rc-major"><a href="http://www.yourwap.com" yourwap="" class="wiki">yourwap</a>
```

```
  </li>
  <li class="rc-major"><a href="http://m.gmail.com" gmail="" class="wiki">gmail</a>
  </li>
  <li class="rc-major"><a href="http://www.wapsilion.com" wapsilion=""
class="wiki">wapsilion</a>
  </li>
<li class="rc-major"><a href="http://wap.oa.yahoo.com/#c1" yahoo="" mail=""
class="wiki">Yahoo Mail</a>
  </li>
  <li class="rc-major"><a href="http://news.bbc.co.uk/1/low" bbc="" class="wiki">BBC</a>
  </li>
  <li class="rc-major"><a href="http://www.vodafone.co.nz" vodafone=""
class="wiki">vodafone</a>
  </li>
<li class="rc-major"><a href="http://www.geocities.com/leftfieldnz" leftfieldnz=""
class="wiki">leftfieldnz</a>
  </li>
</body>
</html>
```

Create an Internet Website

Creating a Website nowadays is pretty simple.

Have a look at my Website at www.webng.com/leftfieldnz

Use View > View Document Source to see how a page is written.

I use a Wordprocessor like Open Office Writer and create the basics in that. I then go File > Save As > HTML Document.

I then use an HTML Editor like Kompozer (or even just a text editor like Windows notepad) and do the fine tuning in there.

For a simple but effective website it is only a matter of writing a few webpages, link them together add some pictures and the upload to your website.

http://www.wikihow.com/Make-a-Website

http://www.wikihow.com/Create-a-Simple-Web-Page-With-HTML

There are plenty of free websites hosts if you do not wish to spend much money.

We currently use www.webng.com they have proved to be very good.

You need a front page which is normally index.html and then maybe a book page.
NB do not use capitals, spaces or odd symbols in a webpage name.

You will also need a folder say called images for the various pictures, and a folder called docs for the various documents you will have.

I like to keep a website very simple and have only two or three clicks to a sale.

So your website will look like;
/docs
sample.pdf
/images
frontcover.jpg
certificate.jpg

In the Root/Main Folder
books.html
index.html
orders.html
enquire.html

If you have a look at Craig's site at www.webng.com/writernz you will get the idea.

Right click on a page and go view source, this will show you the code we have used to create the website.

Logon to your website say www.webng.com and go to the file manager. Create the folders and then upload the webpages, images and documents. Then have a look and see if things have turned out as planned.

Offer the samplebook.pdf you created as a free download.

Another good idea is to sell your products with a Paypal option. Check out www.paypal.com

NB everything in HTML has to open and close, so <b>Bold Text</b> Will open and close bold text.

This is a full page of my website;

```
<!DOCTYPE HTML PUBLIC "-//W3C//DTD HTML 4.01 Transitional//EN"
"http://www.w3.org/TR/html4/loose.dtd">
<HTML>
<HEAD>
        <META HTTP-EQUIV="CONTENT-TYPE" CONTENT="text/html; charset=utf-8">
        <TITLE>Creative Writing and Book Publishing Course</TITLE>
        <META NAME="GENERATOR" CONTENT="OpenOffice.org 2.4  (Linux)">
        <META NAME="CREATED" CONTENT="0;0">
        <META NAME="CHANGED" CONTENT="20081104;434500">
        <META NAME="SDENDNOTE" CONTENT="ARABIC">
        <STYLE TYPE="text/css">
        <!--
                @page { margin: 2cm }
                P { margin-bottom: 0.21cm; font-family: "Times New Roman", serif; font-size:
12pt }
                A:visited { color: #000000; text-decoration: none }
        -->
        </STYLE>
</HEAD>
<BODY LANG="en-GB" VLINK="#000000" DIR="LTR" STYLE="border: none; padding: 0cm">
<div ALIGN=CENTER><FONT COLOR="navy"><FONT FACE="Times New Roman,
serif"><FONT SIZE=6><B>Creative
Writing and Book Publishing Course</B></FONT></FONT></FONT></div>
<p>
```

```html
<strong><div ALIGN="CENTER"><a href="../index.html"> <FONT
SIZE=3>[HOME]</FONT></a><div ALIGN="CENTER"><a href="order.html"><FONT
SIZE=3>[Order]</FONT></a><a href="../inquire.html"> <FONT
SIZE=3>[Enquire]</FONT></a></strong>

<p></div>


</p>

<img src="images/frontcover.jpg" name="Graphic2" align="right" border="0" height="410"
width="280">

<FONT COLOR="#000000"><FONT FACE="Times New Roman, serif"><FONT
SIZE=3><B>Eagle

Productions in association with Nugrow Technologies present their all

New "<I>Creative Writing and Book Publishing
Course".</I></B></FONT></FONT></FONT></div>

<p>

</div>

<FONT COLOR="#000000"><FONT FACE="Times New Roman, serif"><FONT SIZE=3>Get

Cracking and get your book written, completed and published now!
</FONT></FONT></FONT></div>

<p>

</div>

<FONT COLOR="#000000"><FONT FACE="Times New Roman, serif"><FONT SIZE=3><I>We

offer the complete package of helping you write that book within you

and to get it published.</I></FONT></FONT></FONT></div>

<p>

</div>

<FONT COLOR="#000000"><FONT FACE="Times New Roman, serif"><FONT SIZE=3>The

Course is fifteen lessons via email with an input from your Personal

Tutors.</FONT></FONT></FONT></div>

<BR>

</div>

<FONT COLOR="#000000"><FONT FACE="Times New Roman, serif"><FONT SIZE=3>At

the end of the course you will have a published book, if you have a

manuscript ready to go!</FONT></FONT></FONT></div>

<p>

<A HREF="writingpublishcourse.pdf">[Click here to Download Course Outline]</a>
```

```html
</div>

<P STYLE="margin-bottom: 0cm"><FONT FACE="Nimbus Roman No9 L, serif"><FONT
FACE="Times New Roman, serif"><FONT SIZE=3>If

you wish we will issue a Certificate of Participation. Just send the

details of your Name and Address to </FONT></FONT><A
HREF="mailto:leftfieldnz@gmail.com"><FONT FACE="Times New Roman, serif"><FONT
SIZE=3>leftfieldnz at gmail.com</FONT></FONT></A><FONT FACE="Times New Roman,
serif"><FONT SIZE=3>

and we will issue a Certificate.</FONT></FONT></FONT></div>

<P STYLE="margin-bottom: 0cm"><BR>

</div>

<FONT COLOR="#000000"><FONT FACE="Times New Roman, serif"><FONT SIZE=3>Course

Cost $NZ300 or $US200</FONT></FONT></FONT></div>

<form target="paypal" action="https://www.paypal.com/cgi-bin/webscr" method="post">

<input type="hidden" name="cmd" value="_s-xclick">

<input type="hidden" name="hosted_button_id" value="918997">

<input type="image" src="https://www.paypal.com/en_GB/i/btn/btn_cart_LG.gif" border="0"
name="submit" alt="">

<img alt="" border="0" src="https://www.paypal.com/en_US/i/scr/pixel.gif" width="1"
height="1">

</form>


<BR>

</div>

<FONT COLOR="#000000"><FONT FACE="Times New Roman, serif"><FONT SIZE=3>For

more information visit our website <A
HREF="http://www.webng.com/writernz">www.webng.com/writernz</A>

</FONT></FONT></FONT>

</div>

<FONT COLOR="#000000"><FONT FACE="Times New Roman, serif"><FONT SIZE=3>or

email <A HREF="mailto:leftfieldnz@gmail.com">leftfieldnz at gmail.com</A>


</FONT></FONT></FONT>

</div>

<BR>
```

</div>

<FONT COLOR="#000000"><FONT FACE="Times New Roman, serif"><FONT SIZE=3>Pay for the course via Paypal, Visa, Mastercard or a Cheque or of cause Cash</FONT></FONT></FONT></div>

<img src="images/certificate.jpg" name="Graphic233" align="middle" border="0" height="310" width="380">

<FONT COLOR="#000000"><FONT FACE="Times New Roman, serif"><FONT SIZE=3>This a look at the course content;</FONT></FONT></FONT>

<p>

<B>Lesson 1</B>

<p>

INTRODUCTION: </div>

<p>

GETTING STARTED: </div>

<p>

THEN   </div>

<P LANG="en-US" STYLE="margin-bottom: 0cm; line-height: 100%"><FONT COLOR="#000000"><FONT FACE="Times New Roman, serif"><FONT SIZE=3>

     Homework:
</FONT></FONT></FONT>

</div>

<P STYLE="margin-left: 1.27cm; text-indent: -0.76cm; margin-bottom: 0cm">

<B>Lesson 2</B></div>

<p>

What other tips are there?   </div>

<p>

GETTING STARTED   </div>

<p>

WHAT TO WRITE ABOUT?   </div>

<p>

So after all this...   </div>

<P LANG="en-US" STYLE="margin-bottom: 0cm; line-height: 100%"><FONT COLOR="#000000"><FONT FACE="Times New Roman, serif"><FONT SIZE=3>

     Homework:
</FONT></FONT></FONT>

```
</div>

<P LANG="en-US" STYLE="margin-bottom: 0cm; line-height: 100%"><FONT
COLOR="#000000"><FONT FACE="Times New Roman, serif"><FONT SIZE=3><I><B>Lesson
3 <BR>What to do if publisher says 'no'<BR></B></I>Subsidized<BR>Vanity
publishing<BR>Publishing yourself (Self Publishing)<BR>Book
packaging<BR></FONT></FONT></FONT><BR>

</div>

<P LANG="en-US" STYLE="margin-bottom: 0cm; line-height: 100%"><FONT
COLOR="#000000"><FONT FACE="Times New Roman, serif"><FONT SIZE=3><I><B>Lesson
4 <BR>Money matters<BR></B></I>Price Structure<BR>Royalties<BR>Advances<BR>Fee
rather than royalty<BR>tax<BR>Agents<BR> <BR>CONTRACT<BR>Law:
Copyright and Plagiarism big word,
eh!)<I><B><BR></B></I></FONT></FONT></FONT><BR>

</div>

<P LANG="en-US" STYLE="margin-bottom: 0cm; line-height: 100%"><FONT
COLOR="#000000"><FONT FACE="Times New Roman, serif"><FONT SIZE=3><I><B>Lesson
5 <BR>Whos who in the publishers
office<BR></B></I>Publisher<BR>editor<BR>designer<BR>production
manager<BR>sales and marketing<BR><I><B> <BR></B></I>PRODUCING THE
MANUSCRIPT:<BR> <BR>Typing or Word Processor?<BR>number of
copies<BR>disc?<BR></FONT></FONT></FONT><BR>

</div>

<P LANG="en-US" STYLE="margin-bottom: 0cm; line-height: 100%"><FONT
COLOR="#000000"><FONT FACE="Times New Roman, serif"><FONT SIZE=3><I><B>Lesson
6 <BR>Points to remember while you're writing<BR></B></I>style and
consistency<BR>sexism<BR>racism<BR>notes and refs<BR>tables and
figures<BR>photos<BR>drawings<BR>maps,
bibliography<BR></FONT></FONT></FONT><BR>

</div>

<P LANG="en-US" STYLE="margin-bottom: 0cm; line-height: 100%"><FONT
COLOR="#000000"><FONT FACE="Times New Roman, serif"><FONT SIZE=3><I><B>Lesson
7</B></I> <BR><I><B>How to Present the Manuscript?<BR></B></I>Publishing
process.<BR>What will happen to your book<BR></FONT></FONT></FONT><BR>

</div>

<P LANG="en-US" STYLE="margin-bottom: 0cm; line-height: 100%"><FONT
COLOR="#000000"><FONT FACE="Times New Roman, serif"><FONT SIZE=3><I><B>Lesson
```

8
Checking proofs.
</B></I> Marking mistakes clearly

Reading
 Don't rewrite
 Don't worry
</FONT></FONT></FONT>

</div>

<P LANG="en-US" STYLE="margin-bottom: 0cm; line-height: 100%"><FONT COLOR="#000000"><FONT FACE="Times New Roman, serif"><FONT SIZE=3><I><B>Lesson

9</B></I>
<I><B>After publication
</B></I>Author

questionnaire
promotion
launching party?
reviews
remainders

and discounting
</FONT></FONT></FONT>

</div>

<P LANG="en-US" STYLE="margin-bottom: 0cm; line-height: 100%"><FONT COLOR="#000000"><FONT FACE="Times New Roman, serif"><FONT SIZE=3><I><B>Lesson

10
The final word: Review of course so far</B></I></FONT></FONT></FONT></div>

<P LANG="en-US" STYLE="margin-bottom: 0cm; line-height: 100%">

</div>

<P LANG="en-US" STYLE="margin-bottom: 0cm; line-height: 100%"><FONT COLOR="#000000"><FONT FACE="Times New Roman, serif"><FONT SIZE=3><SPAN LANG="zxx"></SPAN></FONT></FONT><FONT FACE="Times New Roman, serif"><FONT SIZE=3>SOME

MORE INFO ON CONTENTS OF COURSE
Other topics covered in this

course (and manuscript) are:

HOW TO WRITE A "DARN"

GOOD NOVEL
HOW TO PRESENT A BOOK PROPOSAL
SELF PUBLISHING
HOW

TO PRESENT A MANUSCRIPT
CONTRACTS
AGENTS
COPYRIGHT
WRITING

FOR CHILDREN

</FONT></FONT></FONT>

</div>

<P STYLE="margin-left: 1.27cm; text-indent: -0.76cm; margin-bottom: 0cm">

<B>Lesson 11</B></div>

<p>

Suggested Software   </div>

<p>

Prepare Manuscript   </div>

<p>

Format Document   </div>

<p>

Font, Layout, Table of Contents, etc   </div>

<P STYLE="margin-left: 2.54cm; text-indent: -0.76cm; margin-bottom: 0cm; line-height: 100%">
<FONT COLOR="#000000"><FONT FACE="Times New Roman, serif"><FONT SIZE=3>Lesson
Conclusion</FONT></FONT></FONT></div>

</div>
<P STYLE="margin-left: 1.27cm; text-indent: -0.76cm; margin-bottom: 0cm">
<B>Lesson 12</B></div>
<p>
Spell Check, Edit and Proof Read document   </div>
<P STYLE="margin-left: 2.54cm; text-indent: -0.76cm; margin-bottom: 0cm; line-height: 100%">
<FONT COLOR="#000000"><FONT FACE="Times New Roman, serif"><FONT SIZE=3>Lesson
Conclusion</FONT></FONT></FONT></div>

</div>
<P STYLE="margin-left: 1.27cm; text-indent: -0.76cm; margin-bottom: 0cm">
<B>Lesson 13</B></div>
<p>
Obtain an ISBN number </div>
<p>
Create Cover   </div>
<p>
Create PDF or DOC   </div>
<p>
Upload to Internet   </div>
<P STYLE="margin-left: 2.54cm; text-indent: -0.76cm; margin-bottom: 0cm; font-weight:
medium">
<FONT COLOR="#000000"><FONT FACE="Times New Roman, serif"><FONT SIZE=3>Lesson
Conclusion</FONT></FONT></FONT></div>
<P STYLE="margin-bottom: 0cm">
</div>
<P STYLE="margin-left: 1.27cm; text-indent: -0.76cm; margin-bottom: 0cm">
<B>Lesson 14</B></div>
<p>
Create a Sample PDF Document </div>

<p>

Create a website </div>

<P STYLE="margin-left: 2.54cm; text-indent: -0.76cm; margin-bottom: 0cm; line-height: 100%">

<FONT COLOR="#000000"><FONT FACE="Times New Roman, serif"><FONT SIZE=3>Lesson

Conclusion</FONT></FONT></FONT></div>

</div>

<P STYLE="margin-left: 1.27cm; text-indent: -0.76cm; margin-bottom: 0cm">

<B>Lesson 15</B></div>

<p>

Publish on www.lulu.com   </div>

<p>

Promote on Google Books, Youtube etc.   </div>

<p>

Order Some Copies of Your Book from Lulu   </div>

<p>

Some Interesting Websites   </div>

<P STYLE="margin-left: 2.54cm; text-indent: -0.76cm; margin-bottom: 0cm; line-height: 100%">

<FONT COLOR="#000000"><FONT FACE="Times New Roman, serif"><FONT SIZE=3>Lesson

Conclusion</FONT></FONT></FONT></div>

<P STYLE="margin-left: 2.54cm; text-indent: -0.76cm; margin-bottom: 0cm; line-height: 100%">

<FONT COLOR="#000000"><FONT FACE="Times New Roman, serif"><FONT

SIZE=3>Certificate

of Participation</FONT></FONT></FONT></div>

</div>

<FONT COLOR="#000000"><FONT FACE="Times New Roman, serif"><FONT

SIZE=3>Creative

Writing Tutor</FONT></FONT></FONT></div>

<div ALIGN=JUSTIFY STYLE="margin-bottom: 0cm; line-height: 100%"><FONT

COLOR="#000000"><FONT FACE="Times New Roman, serif"><FONT SIZE=3>Craig

Lock of Eagle Productions a writer and author and educator</FONT></FONT></FONT></div>

<div ALIGN=JUSTIFY STYLE="margin-bottom: 0cm; line-height: 100%"><FONT

COLOR="#000000"><FONT FACE="Times New Roman, serif"><FONT

SIZE=3>clock@paradise.net.nz</FONT></FONT></FONT></div>

<div ALIGN=JUSTIFY STYLE="margin-bottom: 0cm; line-height: 100%">
</div>

<div ALIGN=JUSTIFY STYLE="margin-bottom: 0cm; line-height: 100%"><FONT COLOR="#000000"><FONT FACE="Times New Roman, serif"><FONT SIZE=3>Publishing Tutor</FONT></FONT></FONT></div>

<div ALIGN=JUSTIFY STYLE="margin-bottom: 0cm; line-height: 100%"><FONT COLOR="#000000"><FONT FACE="Times New Roman, serif"><FONT SIZE=3>Bill Rosoman of Nugrow Technologies a Computer IT Specialist and Writer</FONT></FONT></FONT></div>

<div ALIGN=JUSTIFY STYLE="margin-bottom: 0cm; line-height: 100%"><FONT COLOR="#000000"><FONT FACE="Times New Roman, serif"><FONT SIZE=3>leftfieldnz@gmail.com</FONT></FONT></FONT></div>

<div ALIGN=JUSTIFY STYLE="margin-bottom: 0cm; line-height: 100%">
</div>

<div ALIGN=JUSTIFY STYLE="margin-bottom: 0cm; line-height: 100%"><FONT COLOR="#000000"><FONT FACE="Times New Roman, serif"><FONT SIZE=3>websites</FONT></FONT></FONT></div>

<div ALIGN=JUSTIFY STYLE="margin-bottom: 0cm; line-height: 100%"><FONT COLOR="#000000"><FONT FACE="Times New Roman, serif"><FONT SIZE=3>www.webng.com/writernz</FONT></FONT></FONT></div>

<div ALIGN=JUSTIFY STYLE="margin-bottom: 0cm; line-height: 100%"><FONT COLOR="#000000"><FONT FACE="Times New Roman, serif"><FONT SIZE=3>or
</FONT></FONT></FONT>

</div>

<div ALIGN=JUSTIFY STYLE="margin-bottom: 0cm; line-height: 100%"><FONT COLOR="#000000"><FONT FACE="Times New Roman, serif"><FONT SIZE=3>www.webng.com/leftfieldnz</FONT></FONT></FONT></div>

<div ALIGN=JUSTIFY STYLE="margin-bottom: 0cm; line-height: 100%">
</div>

<div ALIGN=JUSTIFY STYLE="margin-bottom: 0cm; line-height: 100%"><FONT COLOR="#000000"><FONT FACE="Times New Roman, serif"><FONT SIZE=3>TTFN
Bill and Craig</FONT></FONT></FONT></div>

<div ALIGN=JUSTIFY STYLE="margin-bottom: 0cm; line-height: 100%">
</div>

<div ALIGN=JUSTIFY STYLE="margin-bottom: 0cm; line-height: 100%">
</div>

```
</BODY>
</HTML>
```

So it looks like this;

**Creative Writing and
Book Publishing Course**

[HOME]
[Order] [Enquire]

**Eagle Productions in association with
Nugrow Technologies present their all
New "Creative Writing and Book
Publishing Course".**

**Get Cracking and get your book
written, completed and published now!**

*We offer the complete package of
helping you write that book within you
and to get it published.*

**The Course is fifteen lessons via email
with an input from your Personal
Tutors. At the end of the course you
will have a published book, if you have
a manuscript ready to go!**

[Click here to Download Course
Outline]

**If you wish we will issue a Certificate
of Participation. Just send the details of your Name and Address to leftfieldnz at gmail.com
and we will issue a Certificate.**

Course Cost $NZ300 or $US200

**For more information visit our website www.webng.com/writernz or email leftfieldnz at
gmail.com Pay for the course via Paypal, Visa, Mastercard or a Cheque or of cause Cash**

Tips and Tricks

CTRL+ESC	Access Start Menu
CTRL+ALT+DEL	Access Logon and System (Good Place to Kill Not Responding)

ALT+TAB   Rotate between Open Programs

How to make your Desktop Icons Transparent

Go to Control Panel > System, > Advanced > Performance area > Settings button Visual Effects tab
"Use drop shadows for icon labels on the Desktop"

Move your taskbar to a new spot

By default, the Microsoft Windows taskbar, which shows buttons for each of your open windows,
sits at the bottom of your screen. That's fine if you don't open many windows. If you have more
than six or seven windows open at a time, however, the taskbar can become extremely crowded. To
make more room for windows, move your taskbar to the right or left side of the screen, where it will
be displayed vertically, giving you room for more than a dozen windows.

Tip: If you have a widescreen monitor, placing your taskbar on the right or left side of the screen
can make much more efficient use of screen space.

To move your taskbar

Right-click your taskbar. If there is a check mark beside Lock the Taskbar on the shortcut menu,
click Lock the Taskbar to unlock it.

Taskbar shortcut menu with Lock the Taskbar selected

Drag your taskbar to the left, right, or top of your screen. To drag the taskbar, click and hold the
mouse button over the taskbar. Then, while holding down the mouse button, drag the taskbar to its
new location. When the taskbar is in place, release the mouse button.

Move the pointer over an edge of the taskbar until the pointer changes to a double-headed arrow.
Click the mouse button, and drag the edge of the taskbar to widen it. When you can read the
window titles, release the mouse button.

Resized taskbar

Finally, to prevent your taskbar from being accidentally moved, right-click your taskbar, and click
Lock the Taskbar on the shortcut menu.

Resized taskbar with Lock the Taskbar selected on the shortcut menu

Quick Launch Bar

The Quick Launch bar is a list of shortcuts to your favourite programs. You can use the Quick

Launch bar to open programs with a single click, without having to go through the Start menu. Microsoft Windows XP displays the Quick Launch bar by default, so it might already be part of your taskbar. Look for the Quick Launch bar directly to the right of your Start button.

If you have disabled your Quick Launch bar, you can display it by right-clicking your taskbar, clicking Toolbars, and then clicking Quick Launch.

screen saver

Create a personal screen saver using your photos

If you like using a screen saver and have digital photos on your computer, you can easily make your own screen saver using the pictures that you have stored on your PC. You can set up your screen saver in Microsoft Windows to display a slide show of some or all of your pictures when you're not using your computer.

To set up a My Pictures slide show

Right-click on the desktop, and then click Properties.

Desktop shortcut menu with Properties selected

In the Display Properties dialog box, click the Screen Saver tab. Then, click the Screen saver list, and click My Pictures Slideshow.

Disclaimer

The views expressed are not necessarily the views of Bill Rosoman.

Bill Rosoman and Nugrow Technologies disclaims all warranties with regard to Information and Resources available on my Web Site or on this CD, or in any Documentation, including all implied warranties of merchantability and fitness, in no event shall I be liable for any special, indirect or consequential damages or any damages whatsoever resulting from loss of use, data or profits, whether in an Action of contract, negligence or other tortious action, arising out of or in connection with the use or performance of this information.

All rights of the respective software packages, information and resources, and copyright owners is acknowledged.

Easy as Pie!
Bill Rosoman Dip CS
Glen Afton
New Zealand
Phone +64-212335427
Skype, Yahoo IM, MSM IM = leftfieldnz
leftfieldnz@gmail.com
www.webng.com/leftfieldnz

Bill Rosoman Books/Ebooks

The Ultimate Desktop Publishing Book

Desktop Publishing using Free Open Source Software. A Brilliant Book giving You All the Tools and Examples You Need to Create That Masterpiece within You. Creating and publishing a magazine, books, posters, flyers, calendar, menu, award certificates, or business cards could Never Be Easier. Using Free Open Source Software FOSS. Scribus, Open Office, Gimp, Inkscape, Calibre. By Bill Rosoman Dip CS

http://www.lulu.com/product/paperback/the-ultimate-desktop-publishing-book/14847923

The Simple On The Road Cook Book

The Simple On The Road Cook Book. A Useful Easy, Simple and Budget Conscious Guide for Bachelors and other Food Preparation and Cooking Challenged People. Especially if Living in a Confined Space or On The Road.

http://www.lulu.com/content/paperback-book/the-simple-on-the-road-cook-book/8674457

Howto for Windows and Internet Virgins (book)

A Howto for Windows and Internet Virgins using the Windows Operating System. A Beginners Guide to using Window

http://www.lulu.com/content/paperback-book/howto-for-windows-and-internet-virgins/6121427

Te Ao Wiremu, Bill's World

Te Ao Wiremu, Bill's World, Honorary Black, Thirty years on the East Coast. Bill Rosoman spent 29 years living and working on the East Coast of the North Island of New Zealand above Gisborne. This is his yarn about his life there and the funny and not so funny things that happened.

http://www.lulu.com/content/paperback-book/te-ao-wiremu-bills-world/4030752

Get a Life (The Dummies Guide To Life)

The book "Get a Life (The Dummies Guide To Life)", grew out of my brushes with life and my life long study of and fascination with human nature. I also had a bout of cancer in 2006. I find it interesting how people react to big events like finding out you have cancer. Personally I believe you have to take the good with the bad and get on with it. So I decided to write my thoughts down on my laptop and see what comes up! LOL The opinions expressed are mostly my own with help from quotations etc.

http://www.lulu.com/content/paperback-book/get-a-life-%28the-dummies-guide-to-life%29/1262704

http://www.smashwords.com/books/view/31925

Android Tablet Apads How to

Android Tablets Apad How to", Some great Information for the use of Android Tablets. Tablets are the device of the future.

http://www.smashwords.com/books/view/35819

EPUB, How To Write and Publish an Ebook

An ebook, "EPUB, How To Write and Publish an Ebook", using free software (FOSS), Writing and publishing and ebook is quite different from a hard copy book. This ebook gives you all the basic software and knowledge and skills to create your own epics for the modern age.

http://www.smashwords.com/books/view/32052

Puppy Linux Manual

An ebook, "Puppy Linux Manual", Some great Information for the use of Puppy Linux, a Free Operating System which is great on older computers. Puppy Linux is also good for formatting and partitioning hard drives and rescuing data from crash computers.

http://www.smashwords.com/books/view/35818

Bill's Tome

An ebook, "Bill's Tome", All That I Know Life, the Universe, Mortality etc.!

https://www.smashwords.com/books/view/41385

Creative Kiwis, an Amazing Journey

Bill Rosoman and Craig Lock

An ebook, "Creative Kiwis, an Amazing Journey", this book is about the journey of two people in the world of the Internet and Ebook and Book Publishing and Marketing. A massive journey and learning process.

http://www.smashwords.com/books/view/43270

A'holes That I've Known

A look at some of the A'holes I have meet in my life. Life is not always a bed of roses and you have to deal with some not so nice people. Still life is great and you move through life and it's ups and downs. Being confident, articulate and assertive is the way to go, no door mouse for me. LOL

http://www.smashwords.com/books/view/44346

http://www.lulu.com/product/paperback/aholes-that-ive-known/14963987

Don't Say Can't

Don't Say Can't, an ebook about the bad habit of people saying can't, and how we should live in a "Can't Free Zone". Do you continue to bang your head against a brick wall and continually meet the same obstacles of life or do you stop saying can't and branch out in a new and positive direction in your life.

http://www.smashwords.com/books/view/55083

http://goo.gl/C4mD2

Way Outback

Way Outback is a practical guide to going bush way out back in the 21st century as a matter of dropping out financially for self-sufficiency, survival and protection, especially if TSHTF. People do not plan to fail, they just fail to plan.

Ebook

http://goo.gl/Q00sl

Printed Copy

http://goo.gl/mAoEH

Craig Lock Books/Ebooks

A New Dawn

A passionate story of inspiration: hope, faith, peace and especially LOVE for the world and inspired by what I simply term God, the Creative Source of Life itself. That is my legacy to my beloved family...and the world. "But they that wait upon the Lord shall renew their strength, they shall mount up with wings as eagles; they shall run and not be weary; and they shall walk, and not faint." - Isiah 40:31

http://www.lulu.com/product/paperback/a-new-dawn/13399980

RETURN OF THE CHICKENS (e-book)

After that little interlude, I hope every one of you, the "New Safs" enjoy my book....and I hope you don't lynch me when you find me (like Salmon Rushdie) - something fishy going on? Because I believe that a sense of humour definitely helps in the hard but exciting years ahead of living in our "new beloved country".

Quote Unquote": Quotations that I like... very much (book)

This is one of my first manuscripts and a rather short one at that - just like the author. I have also included a separate section on motivational quotes for all salespeople and on business in general (see Part Two). These often helped me in my rather more formal previous commercial career. But even if you are not in business , nor in sales you might find them inspiring (or inspirational) as we journey through the game that is life. I do. ... so time to get right into it / them and get "cracking" or "weaving" as my dear mother would say.

Peace Lives Within (e-book)

These are some notes that I've made recently (from my "red book"), which is forming the basis, the frame-work, the building-blocks for a new manuscript I'm writing. So will share with you and post extracts (hopefully regularly) on my Wordpress blog (craiglock.wordpress.com) as I write it. Hopefully I'll continue getting my "daily dose of inspiration".

https://www.smashwords.com/books/view/43299

http://www.lulu.com/content/e-book/peace-lives-within/9419604

To The End Of The Rainbow (e-book)

Craig has a 'passion' for writing books that tell stories about people doing positive things in this often so hard, sometimes unkind world, occasionally so cruel, yet always amazing world He loves 'telling tales', sharing true stories that leave the reader feeling uplifted, empowered and perhaps hopefully even inspired. Craig loves to try to "test his writing limits and imagination"and is currently writing 'To The End of the Rainbow'. I don't know how my story will end, but I do know how it all began!

http://www.lulu.com/content/e-book/to-the-end-of-the-rainbow/9419597

Angolan Dawn (book)

A true tale of an Angolan migrant miner who goes to 'e'Goli', the big city of gold in South Africa. Also a realistic portrayal of the Angolan conflict in "darkest Africa" through the eyes of a hospital orderly. A moving and realistic novel about the evil and destructiveness of war, as well as the inherent goodness within every human spirit. History, Angola, Southern Africa, Legacy, Gisborne, New Zealand, South Africa, Travel, Africa, War, Politics, Humanity, Conflict, Novel

http://www.lulu.com/content/paperback-book/angolan-dawn/8391177

How to Write a Book and Get Published (book)

Get Cracking and get your book written, completed and published now! We offer the complete package of helping you write that book within you and to get it published. At the end of the book you will have a published book, if you have a manuscript ready to go!

http://www.lulu.com/content/paperback-book/how-to-write-a-book-and-get-published/7313395

The New Rainbow (book)

THE NEW RAINBOW A tale of the many people in the rainbow nation of New South

Africans

http://www.lulu.com/content/paperback-book/the-new-rainbow/7074514

I'LL DO IT MY WAY (book)

Childhood in South Africa, South African Politics and Apartheid and our new life in New Zealand

http://www.lulu.com/content/paperback-book/ill-do-it-my-way/6121816

Handbook for Survival in the Nineties and especially the New Millennium (book)

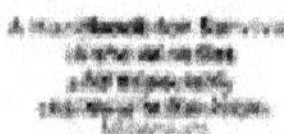

A collection of writings on various subjects to help every man or woman survive in a rapidly changing, uncertain world... after the "easy living and prosperity" of the seventies and eighties. An introductory look at the concepts of success, motivation, attitude, goal setting and stress

https://www.smashwords.com/books/view/43289

http://www.lulu.com/content/paperback-book/handbook-for-survival-in-the-nineties-and-especially-the-new-millenium/1660924

The End of the Line (book)

This is Craig Lock's first novel. A short novel set in "the beloved country". A passionate and heart-breaking tale of South Africa, a true story of the bad old days, but with the hope of the new. "The End Of The Line" could be described as a "faction", a fiction with a serious factual grounding. It is simple, and therefore moving. It gives yet another highly individual portrait of that troubled land, and it does so through a believable and sustained narrative form."

http://www.lulu.com/content/paperback-book/the-end-of-the-line/1630869
https://www.smashwords.com/books/view/42710

Dropped out In Godzone (book)

A new immigrant's impressions of life in provincial New Zealand (after coming from a large city in South Africa) ... and there were one or two rather funny adventures, nay escapades in "Sleepy Hollow" from time to time.

http://www.lulu.com/content/paperback-book/the-end-of-the-line/1630869
https://www.smashwords.com/books/view/42699

Over The Rainbow (book)

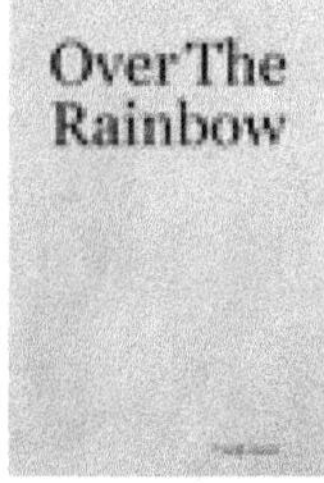

A look at the many colourful peoples, who make up this diverse and vibrant society, as seen through the eyes of a newspaper reporter. Many colourful "vignettes" in this "land of great contrasts" - happy, sad and true, that was the fabric of South African life in the lead up to the historic Democratic Election of 1994. We live in a very complex country of great disparities and extremes, especially in wealth and in living standards. A land of great contradictions: a land of sunshine, a world in one country, a land of laughter in this strange and beautiful place. Much of the laughter from the very people, who have suffered the most and felt the most pain in this strange tormented place of ours. Yes, there is that sadness in the eyes of them too. So to put it simply, South Africa is just one happy, sad land...and I hope that the lives of ALL South Africans will become better in the days ahead.

http://www.lulu.com/content/paperback-book/over-the-rainbow/1265824

Here There and Everywhere

Craig Lock is an extensive world traveller and failed professional emigrater who has spent most of his life's savings on airfares. He is still 'sliding down the razor blade of life', stuck on a deserted (other than a few brilliant rugby players) island at the bottom of the world near Antarctica, where he is 'trying to throw a double six' to get off and go out into the real world - but he doesn't know where! In the style of Bill Bryson, HERE, THERE AND EVERYWHERE tells tales of His hilarious hair-raising adventures in his younger years through 'Grate' Britain and the Continent.

https://www.smashwords.com/books/view/44410

http://www.lulu.com/product/paperback/here-there-and-everywhere/15050656

Notes

Howto for Windows and Internet Virgins.

The Basics in Ung a Windows Computer.
Protection, Maintenance, Programs and their Use, etc.
Using Windows XP and Vista.
Also how the Internet works and how you can use the Internet.

Author Bill Rosoman Dip CS

Published by Bill Rosoman Dip CS
Copies of this book can be ordered from
www.lulu.com/leftfieldnz

First Published 2009

ISBN 978-0-473-14757-0

9 780473 147570